Winning Women's Lacrosse

Kelly Amonte Hiller
with
Ashley Gersuk
Ann Elliott

Human Kinetics

Library of Congress Cataloging-in-Publication Data

Hiller, Kelly Amonte.
  Winning women's lacrosse / Kelly Amonte Hiller with Ashley Gersuk and
Ann Elliott.
      p. cm.
  ISBN-13: 978-0-7360-8000-2 (soft cover)
  ISBN-10: 0-7360-8000-7 (soft cover)
  1. Lacrosse for women. 2. Lacrosse--Coaching. I. Gersuk, Ashley. II.
Elliott, Ann. III. Title.
  GV989.15.H55 2010
  796.347082--dc22

                              2009029050

ISBN-10: 0-7360-8000-7 (print)   ISBN-10: 0-7360-8617-X (Adobe PDF)
ISBN-13: 978-0-7360-8000-2 (print)   ISBN-13: 978-0-7360-8617-2 (Adobe PDF)

Acquisitions Editor: Justin Klug; **Developmental Editor:** Amanda Eastin-Allen; **Assistant Editor:** Laura Podeschi; **Copyeditor:** Ann Prisland; **Proofreader:** Leigh Keylock; **Graphic Designer:** Nancy Rasmus; **Graphic Artist:** Tara Welsch; **Cover Designer:** Keith Blomberg; **Photographer (cover):** John Biever/Sports Illustrated/Getty Images; **Photographer (interior):** Neil Bernstein; **Visual Production Assistant:** Joyce Brumfield; **Photo Production Manager:** Jason Allen; **Art Manager:** Kelly Hendren; **Associate Art Manager:** Alan L. Wilborn; **Illustrator:** Lineworks, Inc.; **Printer:** Versa Press

We thank Loyola Academy in Wilmette, Illinois, for assistance in providing the location for the photo shoot for this book.

Human Kinetics books are available at special discounts for bulk purchase. Special editions or book excerpts can also be created to specification. For details, contact the Special Sales Manager at Human Kinetics.

Printed in the United States of America   10 9 8 7 6 5 4 3 2 1

The paper in this book is certified under a sustainable forestry program.

Human Kinetics
Web site: www.HumanKinetics.com

United States: Human Kinetics
P.O. Box 5076
Champaign, IL 61825-5076
800-747-4457
e-mail: humank@hkusa.com

Canada: Human Kinetics
475 Devonshire Road Unit 100
Windsor, ON N8Y 2L5
800-465-7301 (in Canada only)
e-mail: info@hkcanada.com

Europe: Human Kinetics
107 Bradford Road
Stanningley
Leeds LS28 6AT, United Kingdom
+44 (0) 113 255 5665
e-mail: hk@hkeurope.com

Australia: Human Kinetics
57A Price Avenue
Lower Mitcham, South Australia 5062
08 8372 0999
e-mail: info@hkaustralia.com

New Zealand: Human Kinetics
Division of Sports Distributors NZ Ltd.
P.O. Box 300 226 Albany
North Shore City
Auckland
0064 9 448 1207
e-mail: info@humankinetics.co.nz

                                                                    E4714

To Lewie, aka The Captain

Contents

Acknowledgments   vii

Introduction: Attitude and Focus of a Champion   ix

Key to Diagrams   xv

PART I   Individual Skills

1   Profile of a Successful Player   **3**

2   Developing Essential Skills   **9**

3   Developing Offensive Skills   **29**

4   Developing Defensive Skills   **45**

PART II   Team Play

5   Team Attacking   **61**

6   Team Defense   **71**

7   Team Breaks and Transitions   **81**

PART III Specialty Skills

8 **Field Players**   **91**

9 **Goalkeepers**   **103**

PART IV Mastering the Game

10 **Situational Drills**   **117**

11 **Stick Tricks**   **151**

12 **Conditioning Drills**   **171**

13 **Maximizing Practice Time**   **183**

About the Author   191

Acknowledgments

This book has provided an exciting opportunity to put a coaching philosophy on paper, and there are a number of people who contributed their time and effort to make the book a success.

Special thanks to Lindsey Munday, Kristen Boege, Caitlin Jackson, and Hilary Bowen for your lax knowledge and valuable contributions throughout the process.

Thank you to Margaret Totaro, Jennifer Caldwell, Cristina Couri, Clare Nelson-Johnson, Grace Dooley, Grace Bowen, and Meghan Brady for participating in the photo shoot, and to Loyola Academy for allowing us to use your facility.

Thank you to the Northwestern University Athletic Department for your support.

Last, but certainly not least, thank you to Jaclyn Murphy and the Friends of Jaclyn Foundation for teaching us the most important lacrosse and life lesson of all: "Live in the Moment. Play in the Moment."

Introduction

Attitude and Focus of a Champion

Coaches and players tend to focus on the physical components of the game of lacrosse. Physical skills—stick skills, positioning, attack and defense concepts, conditioning, and others—are certainly essential to success on the lacrosse field. Those skills are the primary focus of this book. Champions and true championship teams, though, evolve when those physical skills are coupled with a focus on the mental components of the game.

Attitude and mental focus are truly x-factors—the differences between a good team and a great team, between a good player and a great player, between making it to a championship game and winning that championship. Following are a few key ideas to help a good player become great and a good team become a championship team. Attitude and mental focus can take all physical skills to the next level.

Positive Attitude

Confidence, beginning with the individual and fostered by the coach, is one of the most fundamental attributes a player at any level can possess. Confidence is the true metric of a great player and of a great team, and it can very quickly spread from individual to team. When a player has confidence, it tends to perpetuate itself and can create a domino effect: That player is more likely to achieve or master something new, gain more confidence, and begin to project that energy on those around her. In turn, a confident player is more likely to support her teammates and foster their confidence.

A great team consists of confident individuals, from starting players to the end of the bench; individual player confidence can quickly become collective team confidence. When players or a team have confidence in themselves, they are more likely to believe in themselves and in their team. A player who believes in herself and in her team can be nearly unstoppable. A team that believes in themselves will be able to accomplish things they may have never thought possible.

It is the coach who initially sets the positive tone and continues to foster this mentality. Every coach has a style and unique approach to imparting knowledge to players. However, an overall positive coaching style is the most effective. Positive attitudes foster confidence and belief in self and in teammates, especially among female athletes.

Ultimately, however, positivity, confidence, and belief must come from players. In a game, the players have ultimate control over what happens on the field, and a teammate is one of the most influential people on the field. Positive reinforcement and encouragement from a teammate on the field can be every bit as effective as from a coach. Coaches must reinforce how essential it is for the positive attitude to be exercised and perpetuated by players. A successful team is made up of players who can maintain a positive, confident attitude throughout the natural trials of a given season.

Team Unity

Team unity evolves from players who share a common attitude and belief, something unique that defines them and sets their team apart from others. An effective way to spark team unity is to develop and define a team theme. The theme can be simple, but it will bring to mind what the team stands for. The theme has a specific and deeper meaning to players and can serve as a constant source of motivation. Players will identify with the theme as their personal and collective purpose for playing—and for playing harder. A team theme facilitates the development of common attitudes and beliefs and serves as a reminder that players are a part of a united group of individuals with a specific purpose.

Here are a few questions that will help in developing team themes:

- What are your team's core values? Outwork the opposing team? Make smart decisions on the field?

- What makes you different from every other team?
- Is there something that defines this particular season? Is your team young? Are you all veterans?
- Do you have a specific goal? Improve on last year's record? Earn a league championship?

Team themes are often secret and are something only the team understands. The theme can be in a different language, coded, or initialed—something that an outsider would not understand.

Using What You Have

Every team is different and every season is different. Personnel changes and coaches change. Players and coaches need to acknowledge from the start that changes will occur from year to year.

Each year, coaches and players need to figure out what is unique about that specific team. This year's team will be different from those in years past: Graduating players will move on, new players will join the team, and new players will step up as leaders. If coaches and players are able to pinpoint the team's uniqueness from the beginning, they will be better able to create an environment and a game plan that uses and maximizes the specific resources of the team.

With that said, certain little things can be developed and emphasized with any combination of personnel. These little things are assets that can be controlled and amount to a much greater importance: hard work, effort, 50–50 balls. Every person on the team directly controls her own effort and hard work. These little things are attributes that should be emphasized on a team regardless of any season-specific variables: skill level, experience, win–loss record, point in the season, and so on. Hard work and effort transcend personnel, skill, and experience level.

Appreciation

Above all else, the goal of lacrosse is to have fun, regardless of players' level of skill—youth, high school, collegiate, or international. A team that has fun is far more likely to achieve their potential.

A team plays a limited number of games throughout a given season, and there is only one championship game. There are far more practice and preparation hours than game-time hours, and players need to appreciate this time as well. A team that truly enjoys their time playing lacrosse will become more united, more energetic, and more determined.

Here are some keys to help create a fun and energetic team environment:

• Change up team practices. It is helpful to do new drills rather than the same ones over and over.

• Use competition to get a team energized and having fun. Nearly any drill can incorporate a competitive element. Players will get excited if they are able to scrimmage every once in a while as well.

• Listen to the team. Every team typically has captains or specific leaders; coaches should be in tune with these leaders and aware of when team members may be tired or in need of an extra spark. It is normal for a team to get tired at certain points throughout the season, and these times can provide opportunities to spend practices doing something fun or different.

Preparation for Competition

Preparation is a key to success on the lacrosse field because it gives players the tools to succeed in a game situation. The more prepared players are when they go into a game, the more familiar they will be with the elements of the game, and the more equipped they will be to respond and execute. Players will eventually reach a point at which various skills and situations are second nature to them.

Here are some key elements of preparation:

• Game speed. Practice drills need to be executed at game speed. Anything that can be done to simulate a game situation will increase players' preparation. For example, drills should be done on the move, shots should be executed at game speed, and defensive communication should have the same urgency as it would in a game. If a coach is able to create a gamelike environment in practice, players will be physically and mentally prepared to execute the same skills and concepts in the game situation.

• Repetition. Practice makes perfect. When players correctly execute the same skills and concepts over and over, they become increasingly comfortable and more likely to execute in game situations.

• Visualization. If a player can imagine executing a certain skill, concept, or game situation correctly, she will be more likely to execute it when the actual opportunity arises. For example, a shooter should visualize a situation in which she cuts through the 8-meter area, receives a pass, sights the goalie's position in the net, finds an open spot, and shoots the ball into the space for a goal. If a player has imagined this sequence numerous times, it will feel more natural when the scenario presents itself in practice and ultimately in a game.

• Extra work. A player can directly control how much extra work she puts into her game. Extra work can and will take any player's game to the next level. Playing wall ball, emphasizing fitness, and watching game film are examples of extra work that a player can do to contribute to her game. No matter how skilled a player becomes, there is unlimited potential to how much higher she can raise the bar with extra work.

These are just a few ideas and concepts. No matter whether a coach chooses to follow some of these ideas, or others, it is essential to address, foster, and emphasize ways for individuals and the team to maintain mental toughness. Doing so will make the difference between being good and being great. There is no single recipe for success in the game of lacrosse, but a positive attitude, team unity, use of team resources, appreciation, and preparation are key ingredients of success.

Key to Diagrams

(A)	Attacker
(D)	Defender
(G) (G)	Goalie
(M) (M)	Midfielder
P	Passer
S	Shooter
X or (1)–(7), **1**–**7**	Players
Xo or ◯₀, ●₀	Players with ball
———	Player movement
- - - - - - -	Ball movement
	Numbers indicate order of movement

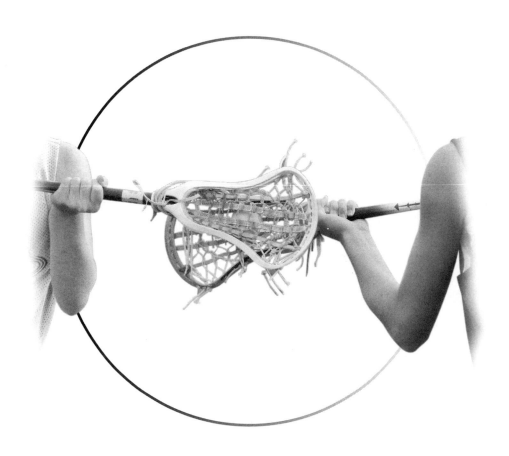

PART I
Individual Skills

Profile of a Successful Player

A lacrosse field is broken into three zones, each of which is covered by a group of position-specific players: attackers, midfielders, defenders, and the goalkeeper. In each of the three zones, position groups possess specific and unique responsibilities. An understanding of each position and the respective zone responsibilities will set a solid foundation upon which to build an increased understanding of lacrosse as a whole. This chapter will provide an introduction to common and favorable lacrosse player characteristics, field setup, and the positions covered by each player on the field.

Common Player Characteristics

Good lacrosse players come in various shapes and sizes, at all ages and levels of experience. Successful lacrosse players at all levels tend to share certain characteristics. The following are a few, but certainly not all, favorable lacrosse characteristics.

Athleticism   Lacrosse is a sport that incorporates many physical and mental skills, including eye–hand coordination, speed, quickness, strength, endurance, and accuracy. Many of these skills are found in various sports. A good athlete with little to no lacrosse-specific experience often can adapt quickly to the game of lacrosse.

Speed   Lacrosse is a game that rewards speed, quickness, and endurance. Some positions require more quickness or more endurance than others, but a good lacrosse player will have a combination of all three. Attacking and defensive positions require significant quickness and speed; the midfield position requires endurance as well as speed. Speed is a player characteristic that can provide a considerable advantage on the lacrosse field.

Field and Positioning Awareness   Lacrosse shares many athletic skills and concepts with sports such as soccer, field hockey, basketball, and ice hockey. Each of these sports has similar offensive and defensive concepts that require an understanding and awareness of positioning and space. For example, an attacker must be aware of her positioning relative to the goal, to her teammates, and to the defenders. A defender must be aware of her positioning relative to the goal, the opposing attackers, and her defensive teammates. Many players who have experience in the aforementioned sports are able to transition well into lacrosse because of their field awareness.

Attacking and Defensive Concepts Awareness   As mentioned, lacrosse shares many concepts with soccer, field hockey, basketball, and ice hockey. The same concepts of space, positioning, and field awareness are required for executing offensive and defensive lacrosse concepts. On attack, players must use the space in the zone, support the ball carrier, and move to create space. On defense, players must cover the space in the zone, support the on-ball defender, and constantly slide and shift around the zone. A player with experience in a similar sport will benefit from an understanding of general attacking and defensive concepts that translate onto the lacrosse field.

Willingness to Learn Perhaps above all else, a player with a strong work ethic and willingness to learn and improve will be most likely to succeed on the lacrosse field.

Positions and Position-Specific Characteristics

The lacrosse field is divided into three zones: defensive zone, attacking zone, and midfield zone. The 40-yard (36.6 m) defensive zone begins with the 10-yard (9.1 m) area behind the defensive goalkeeper and ends at the defensive restraining line, which is 30 yards (27.4 m) from the goal line. The 40-yard attacking zone begins at the offensive restraining line and ends with the 10-yard area behind the opponent's goalkeeper. The midfield zone consists of the 40-yard area between the two restraining lines. There are 12 players on the field at a time: 11 field players and a goalie. Only 7 field players are allowed in the defensive or attacking zones at any given time. The 4 remaining players must stay in the midfield, behind the restraining line. If more than 7 players are in the defensive or attacking zones, the team has violated the offsides rule.

The traditional style of field positioning designates three defenders (point, cover point, and third man), three attackers (first home, second home, and third home), and five midfielders (right and left defensive wing, right and left attack wing, and center). This is not the most effective lineup structure. The currently used lineup and positioning structure is simple: four defenders, four attackers, and three midfielders (figure 1.1). This setup eliminates any confusion about which players go over the restraining line and which do not. The current structure organizes the team but does not limit them. For example, the traditional style of positioning designates a certain midfielder as left attack wing and another as right attack wing. This limits the players to specific sides of the field; the current positioning structure merely designates the players as midfielders, allowing them more freedom to adapt to a game situation. It is unrealistic to assume that a player will only play on a specific side of the field. Certain game circumstances may even force attackers into

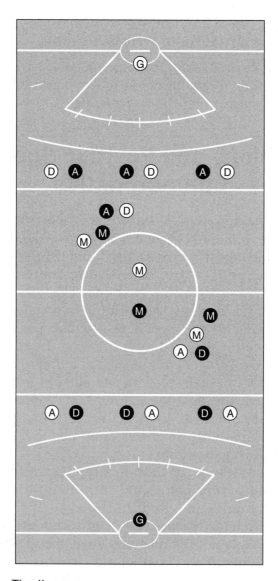

FIGURE 1.1   The lineup.

the defensive zone or defenders into the attacking zone. Although certain players may specialize as attackers or defenders, it is critical that all field players are comfortable in each of the field's three zones: defense, attack, and midfield.

Four Defenders   The four defenders are the core of the defense and should understand their team's defense thoroughly. These players are the lead communicators—along with the goalie—and should also provide the most energy in the defensive zone. They will be well rested, more so than the midfielders who have just transitioned into the defense from the attacking and midfield zones.

Defenders typically remain in the defensive and midfield zones, behind the offensive restraining line. However, if a defender carries the ball out of the defensive zone during a transition play, she should be confident and comfortable enough to continue through the midfield and take the ball over the offensive restraining line and into the attacking zone. In this situation, one of the attackers or midfielders must remain behind the restraining line until the defender comes back over the line. Midfielders need to communicate with each other when they see a defender cross into the attacking zone to avoid being charged with an offsides.

Four Attackers The four attackers are the core of the offense and should understand their team's attack completely. Attackers control the tempo of the game, when to go to goal and when to settle the ball. Attackers are goal scorers and should have good stick skills. In the midfield, attackers make supporting cuts toward the ball carrier. Attackers are more rested than midfielders and must help bring the ball down the field during transition.

After a turnover in their offensive zone, attackers must redefend all the way to the restraining line. Attackers can cause many turnovers by riding, or putting pressure on the other team's defenders and midfielders as they transition the ball upfield.

Three Midfielders Depending on the level of play, midfielders will often be a team's best athletes and ball carriers. These three players are required to play both offense and defense, and they often are the players who carry the ball in the midfield or make midfield passes. Midfielders must know their team's offensive and defensive schemes because they participate in both. Midfielders should be good decision makers and well conditioned.

Goalie A goalie is the anchor of a team's defense and often serves as the initiator of a team's offense. Goalie play can be the defining factor between two teams. It is very difficult for a team to be successful without good goalie play. It is a common misconception that the goalkeeper position is the best fit for a player who is not as fast, athletic, or skilled as her teammates. A typical goalie is athletic and quick, is mentally tough and resilient, has good stickwork, has good hands and reactions, and is aggressive and directive. These characteristics are similar to those found in a top field player. See chapter 9 for more information on the goalie's role.

Roles Within the Team

A lacrosse team can have anywhere from 15 to 35 players on the roster, depending on the level, available player pool, and preference of the coaching staff. Regardless of a team's roster size, there are only 12 positions to fill on the field, so there are extra players to serve as reserves. Only 12 players can start a game, and only 12 players can play at any given time. It is the responsibility of the coaching staff to determine which players fit best in a starting role and which fit best as reserves. Starting players are those who make up the unit the coach believes will best set the tone as a game begins and will be most capable of collectively executing the game plan. Reserves are those who fill a supporting role when the starters need rest, who are not properly executing the game plan, or who enter when the flow of the game requires adjustment.

Understanding the importance of each player's role on the team is essential. As described earlier, lacrosse requires great speed and endurance. One of the most difficult capabilities for a player to master is the ability to execute proper skills and decisions when she is tired. It is rare for a player, at any level, to be capable of playing a full game at maximum speed and potential. When a player comes into the game as a reserve, she offers rested legs and a fresh perspective on the game. Reserves have had the opportunity to watch from the sidelines and absorb game-specific feedback from the coach. Reserve players are essential to the success of a team.

It is also crucial for each player to understand her designated role on the team. The coach is responsible for communicating with players about their roles, and players are responsible for accepting their roles and maximizing their contributions to the team's success. It is healthy for reserves to continue to improve and work to maximize their role on the team. Hard-working reserves will push both starters and other reserves to work harder and get better. Even if a reserve's role does not change, her hard work will have had a direct and tangible impact on the team's betterment. Starters, too, must work hard, continue to improve, and avoid complacency, especially as their teammates continue to progress around them. It is to the absolute benefit of any team to have both starters and reserves who can contribute to a game. The most successful teams are those with depth.

Developing Essential Skills

This chapter breaks down the various stick skills associated with the game of lacrosse. To execute each of these skills, players need to understand and master the basics of proper stick handling, which will facilitate an understanding of shooting, passing, cradling, protection, and deception. Revisiting basic stick-handling concepts will often improve the execution of more advanced skills.

Stick Handling

Basic stick-handling concepts are referred to in this chapter as the basics. As isolated concepts, the basics seem quite simple, but they provide a foundation for the successful execution of more advanced skills. In order to shoot, pass, cradle, and protect, a player needs to maintain an angle on her stick, drop her top hand, face the head of her stick toward the target, and keep her grip loose, her wrists relaxed and flexible, and her arms away from her body. If practiced, the basics will become second nature and will significantly impact a player's ability to execute.

Maintain an Angle on the Stick   By maintaining an angle on the stick, a player allows the ball to easily sit and stay in the stick. To create a good angle on the stick, the player's bottom hand should be raised about a foot (.3 m) away from her belly button (figure 2.1). This will ensure that the bottom hand is farther away than the top hand from the player's body, thus creating an angle on the stick. This concept may seem simple, but it is very important in the execution of passes and shots. The angle is determined by the bottom hand, which is one foot away from the player's belly button. Every player is different, so there is no set degree of measurement for the angle.

FIGURE 2.1   Maintaining an angle on the stick.

Drop the Top Hand   It is recommended that beginners drop the top hand about 4 to 5 inches (10.2-12.7 cm) down from the head of the stick (figure 2.2*a*). A lower top hand facilitates increased power on passes and shots by creating torque. A lower top hand also creates an increased range of motion, making it easier to move the stick around when cradling. Beginners often drop their top hands too low, limiting their control and ability to protect their stick, pass, and shoot. When a player becomes more experienced, she can drop her top hand even lower on the stick (figure 2.2*b*). The exact location of the bottom hand will vary depending on the player's comfort level. A higher top hand increases control, and a lower top hand increases power and flexibility. It is important for each player to find the most comfortable hand placement to balance control and power.

FIGURE 2.2   Dropping the top hand.

Face the Head of the Stick Toward the Target   The head of the stick should be directly above the player's shoulder, and the head of the stick should always face the player's target (figure 2.3, *a-b*). This is called the triple-threat position: It allows a player to pass, shoot, and cradle from the same starting position (figure 2.4, *a-b*). If the bottom hand on the stick is too close to the body, it becomes difficult to keep the head of the stick facing the target, thus eliminating the ability to pass, shoot, or score at any time. If a player's stick faces the target at all times, she is a threat at all times. It is important to use the same starting stick position each time.

FIGURE 2.3   Triple-threat position: facing the head of the stick toward the target.

FIGURE 2.4 Triple-threat position: *(a)* cradling; *(b)* passing or shooting.

Keep the Grip Loose—But Not Too Loose The stick should sit at the base of the player's fingers (top of palm), not on the lower palm. With the stick sitting at the base of the fingers, the tips of the fingers of the top hand should wrap around the stick. The thumb should always be on the shaft (figure 2.5). The way a player holds her stick when she is about to take a shot is the grip she should have on her stick at all times. Although players tend to change their grip from cradling to shooting, it is unnecessary; a grip change wastes precious time. More advanced players should develop the ability to move the stick quickly in their hands, almost rolling it in their fingertips.

FIGURE 2.5 Keeping a loose grip.

Keep the Wrists Relaxed and Flexible   It is important that players keep their wrists relaxed and flexible at all times. This will allow for coordination, range of motion, and rhythm when cradling. Relaxed and flexible wrists allow a player to pass, shoot, or cradle at any time. When a player is using more advanced stickwork, this will become very relevant.

Keep the Arms Away From the Body   Players often think that keeping their arms close to their bodies will help them protect their sticks. This is not the case. It is essential that a player keep her arms away from her body. Both top and bottom arms should be away from the player's torso and waist. The exact distance will depend on her size and comfort; arms should be a comfortable distance away, but close enough so that the player's elbows are still bent, and she is able to maintain control of the stick. This will allow for range of motion when cradling and using more advanced stickwork, and will provide better protection. If a player keeps her arms away from the body, she will have harder and more accurate passes and shots.

As players learn and practice the basics, it is extremely important for them to emphasize the use of both hands. Basic lacrosse skills should be developed with both the right and left hands, dominant and nondominant. Players who are well practiced with both hands will be more effective, especially as they reach higher and more competitive levels.

Shooting and Passing

After a player has become comfortable with the basics of stick handling and is able to control the ball, she is ready to transition into the next steps: passing and shooting. Lacrosse is a team sport that requires effective ball movement from one player to another. There are two parts to the successful execution of a pass: the pass and the reception. The successful transition of possession from one player to another must begin with a good pass.

The ultimate goal of lacrosse is to score goals. The more goals a team can score, the more likely they are to win a game. Similarly, the more times a player is able to capitalize on a scoring opportunity, the more likely her team is to win. There are a limited number of scoring opportunities in a game, and players need to be able to maximize the opportunities they are given.

If a player maintains good form when she passes or shoots, she will maximize the power and accuracy of every pass and shot—and increase the chance and frequency of successful execution. Following are the elements of good shooting form.

• When shooting, make sure your weight starts on the back foot, with your feet shoulder width apart and your front foot planted.

• Keep your arms—both hands and elbows—away from your body, as described in the basic stick-handling section. The player's elbows should be bent; the exact distance away from the body will depend on the specific player.

• Keep your hands approximately 12 inches (.3 m) apart on the stick (figure 2.6a). If your hands are too close together, you will not have enough control over your stick. If your hands are too far apart, you will lose flexibility and power on the shot. Although each player's comfort distance will be slightly different, 12 inches is a general guideline for good shooting form.

• As you shoot, shift your weight from the back foot to the front foot. Simultaneously, rotate your hips, torso, and shoulders toward the target. The shift of weight from front to back, coupled with the rotation of the hips, torso, and shoulders, will bring power into your shot.

• Use a push-pull motion when shooting. Pull the bottom hand down and across the body to the opposite hip. Simultaneously, push or drive your top hand forward, with the head of the stick toward the target (figure 2.6b). The bottom hand should pull across to the other side of your body until the top hand is full extended toward the target. Ultimately, the top hand will follow through, with the head of the stick, to the outside of your planted front foot, on the opposite side of the body.

• As your top and bottom hands engage in the push-pull motion, snap your wrists forward toward the target.

• Transfer your weight from back to front and rotate your torso and hips forward toward the target. A shot's power comes from your legs, hips, and torso. This motion, the torso twist, occurs as you transfer your weight from back to front and rotates your torso and hips forward toward the target. The weight transfer or torso twist should occur simultaneously as your hands push-pull and follow through toward their target. When players are first becoming comfortable with the torso twist, they should overemphasize it. The torso twist is the origin of a shot's power.

- Release the ball after pulling with your bottom hand, pushing with your top hand, and driving the head of your stick toward the target. The stick should follow through to the outside of the planted foot, on the opposite side of the body (figure 2.6c).

The player must aim the head of her stick toward the target, release the ball when it faces the target, and follow through with the head of the stick toward the target and ultimately to the opposite side of the body. The shooting form should flow succinctly because each of the elements must happen simultaneously. As the player's weight transfers from back to front, the torso twists, the arms push-pull, and the wrists snap, all toward the target. After the ball is released, the head of the stick should follow through to the outside of the planted foot, on the opposite side of the body.

FIGURE 2.6 Shooting and passing form: *(a)* starting position, *(b)* release point, and *(c)* follow-through.

Shooting Considerations

There are unique considerations for outside shots and inside shots. A shot is considered to be outside when a player shoots from beyond 6 meters from the goal. When a player takes an outside shot, she should change the plane of her shot. It is particularly important to be deceptive on an outside shot because the goalkeeper has more time to react. The head of the stick should be hidden behind the player's body until the last second before she takes the shot (figure 2.7). She also needs to change the level of her shot. For example, if the player starts her shot from up high, she should change the plane of her shot and shoot low. If the stick is high, the player should drive the shot down low. If the stick is low, the player should shoot up high. She should use the torso twist on outside shots to generate power. Sometimes increased power leads to less accuracy. If a player finds her shots are going wide, she should decrease the power of the shot to allow for more accuracy.

FIGURE 2.7 Shooting considerations: hiding the head of the stick.

When a player shoots from the inside, closer than 6 meters from the goal, accuracy becomes more important than speed. To increase accuracy, a player should shorten up her shooting form and move from the traditional torso twist, which is used to draw power, to a wrist or snap shot (figure 2.8, *a-c*). A shot that uses a shorter windup, less of a follow-through, and a wrist snap provides more accuracy and better protection. Players must remember to use fakes on inside shots to move the goalie but should keep them simple. One fake is sufficient. Shoulder fakes are more effective than stick fakes on inside shots because stick fakes can take a player out of her triple-threat position; this wastes time inside the crowded 8-meter area.

To be an effective shooter, a player must look at the goal to see where the goalie is positioned and how she is playing. Is she right-handed or left-handed? Is she playing high up on the crease or back on the goal line? Is she tall or short? These are all questions for a shooter to consider before she takes a shot. The best spot to shoot is at the goalie's offside (nondominant) hip, below the hip and above the ankle. For example, if the goalie

FIGURE 2.8 Shooting considerations: shortened form.

is right-handed, shoot below her lower left hip. This is why it is important to know if the goalie is right-handed or left-handed.

Players should avoid aiming directly for the corners of the net because every shooter has a natural margin of error. If a player maximizes the percentage of shots that are on net, she will maximize her chances of scoring. If a player aims directly for the corners, her margin of error will cause some shots to fall outside the frame of the net. Players should aim between 6 to 8 inches (15.2-20.3 cm) inside the post. If the shot is 4 inches (10.2 cm) off the mark in any direction, for example, it will still be within the frame of the net. Players should pick a specific piece of the net and aim for it.

Players have the choice to shoot high, low, or even on the ground. Shots on the ground, or bounce shots, can be very effective: They generate a change of direction as they hit the ground, and the ultimate direction of the ball can be difficult for a goalie to anticipate. If a player chooses to shoot a bounce shot, the ball should bounce between 1 and 2 feet (.3 and .6 m) in front of the goalie's feet. This distance gives the ball enough time to change direction, but not too much time to allow the goalie to easily adjust her positioning to react to the change. Regardless of where a player shoots, she must not telegraph the shot. This concept is discussed further in the Deception section later in this chapter.

Players must be familiar with the conditions of the field and take them into account as they attempt to take shots. If the field is muddy, the ball will likely stick to the ground, which makes a bounce shot less effective. Does the ball bounce well? Does it skid? Both shooters and goalkeepers should be aware of how field conditions will affect shots.

Players need to practice their shots on the move and at game speed. It is rare for a player to be given the opportunity to shoot while standing still during a game. When a player shoots on the move, she must keep her feet moving and her speed at a maximum. If a player slows her feet, she may give a defender the opportunity to make a check or regain defensive positioning. The player should continue moving toward the goal and make sure her momentum is going forward. It is important for the player to shoot overhand, never lose sight of the target, and be aware of the defensive pressure. Shooting on the move can be effective because it forces the goalkeeper to move across the crease, making it significantly more difficult for her to get set and make a save.

Passing Considerations

A pass requires many of the same concepts and considerations as a shot. A well-executed pass is contingent on the ability of the passer to execute a good pass, and the ability of the receiving player to assist the passer and maintain possession of the ball.

A player should aim the ball at the other player's stick. Generally speaking, the stick will be on the player's strong side, 6 to 8 inches (15.2-20.3 cm) away from her head. It is important for the passer to sight the target before making a pass because sometimes the receiving player may ask for the ball in a different location than usual. Just as when she is shooting, a player needs to keep her feet moving as she passes the ball. If the passer follows these guidelines, she will increase the chances of her teammate successfully receiving the pass.

Just as there are considerations to be made by the passer, there are certain guidelines the player who receives the pass needs to follow to help ensure a well-executed pass. The receiving player must present the head of her stick to the passer, which shows where she would like to receive the ball (figure 2.9). The receiving player should also be moving her feet at all times and should receive the pass on the move. The receiving player should also communicate, verbally and nonverbally, with the passer, to indicate her readiness to receive the ball. As the ball comes into the receiving player's stick, the receiver should use soft hands, as if she is catching a breakable egg, to best receive the ball and maintain possession.

FIGURE 2.9 Ready to recieve the pass.

Cradling and Protection

Possession is probably the most important variable in the game of lacrosse. Most often, the team that is able to possess the ball longer than the other team will win the game. When a specific player has possession of the ball, it is her responsibility to maintain possession and control the ball by cradling and protecting her stick.

Cradling refers to a coordinated movement of the arms to control the ball in a player's stick. The concept of cradling is similar to that of dribbling in basketball or stick handling in hockey, but the ball does not leave the player's stick as a basketball leaves a player's hands or a puck leaves the hockey player's stick. Fifty percent of effective stick protection stems from sound cradling form and smooth stick movement. Note that a number of the keys to cradling are also keys to the basics.

• As described in the basics, shooting, and passing sections, your arms should stay away from the body as they cradle. The bottom hand should stay away the body, about a foot (.3 m) away from the belly button, ensuring that you maintain an angle on the stick. As also illustrated in the basics, the head of the stick should be directly over your shoulder.

• When you cradle the ball, you must maintain the triple-threat position. For the most part, your stick should always face the target. There is a misconception that when cradling, the player should move the stick all the way across to the other side of the body. This is not the most efficient way to cradle. When cradling, the top hand pushes the stick up and turns it slightly. The bottom hand is relatively quiet, allowing the stick to move freely through the bottom fingers as the top hand controls the movement (figure 2.10). Cradles should be small and quick, allowing for a constant triple-threat position.

FIGURE 2.10 Cradling form.

• Your feet should always be moving when cradling. When you stop your feet, you immediately become vulnerable to a defender. A stationary attacker is much less of a threat than a moving attacker.

• You should practice various cradling points. Although a player will often cradle over her strong-side shoulder (figure 2.11*a*), there are various cradling points with different purposes. For example, a player can cradle in front of her face for increased protection (figure 2.12*a*), or a player can cradle on the opposite side of her body to avoid a defender on her strong side (figures 2.11*b* and 2.12, *b-c*). A player can also cradle high or cradle closer to the ground (figure 2.12, *d-e*). Different cradling points can help with more advanced stickwork. No matter which cradling position you use, you must return to the triple-threat position before you shoot or pass.

To maintain possession, it is essential for a player to protect her stick from defenders. If a player can protect her stick, it will be very difficult for a defender to check the ball out of the player's stick and regain possession. Good stick skills allow for good stick protection. A player needs to be able to move her stick from high to low on both sides of her body. A tenacious defender will challenge a player all around her body; the more dynamic a player is in her ability to move her stick from left to right and from high to low, the more difficult it will be for a defender to

FIGURE 2.11 Cradling: *(a)* strong side; *(b)* weak side.

FIGURE 2.12 Various cradling points.

check the player's stick. The following list includes tips that will help a player protect her stick from a defender.

- Keep your arms away from your body.

- Keep your body between your stick and the defender. Your shoulder should be lined up with the middle of the defender's chest. The game of women's lacrosse prevents a defender from going through a player's body to reach the opponent's stick. If you keep your body between your stick and the defender, you have protected your stick because the defender will not be able to reach the stick without going all the way around your body. If you line up your shoulder with the middle of the defender's chest, you have created the largest possible distance between the defender and the protected stick (figure 2.13, *a-c*).

- Keep your head up and on a swivel. It is essential that you be able to see your open teammates and their defenders at all times. If your head is down, you cannot make an open pass or see a defender's check coming.

- Stand your ground and protect. Stand tall, keep your shoulders up, and keep your stick back. If your head and shoulders are up, it is not necessary for you to move your stick frantically to protect it.

There are also specific considerations for protection on the move and protection while in traffic.

Protection on the Move To make a move on a defender, a player must protect her stick on the approach. The stick must stay back, behind the player's body, as she approaches a defender, not in front or to the side. It may seem natural for the stick to come forward because the body's momentum is going forward, but this will make a player vulnerable to checks and take her out of the triple-threat position. It is important that a player use her body to shield her stick from a check.

 TIP If a player's bottom hand is loose, the ball will not fall out of her stick if she is bumped by a defender.

After the attacking player beats her defender, the rules change. The player must bring her stick in front of her body for at least a few cradles until she has created space between herself and the defender. Even when the stick is in front of a player's body, it is

FIGURE 2.13 Protection.

still important that she move the stick around for protection. The stick should change levels, and the player's head should remain on a swivel so she can stay aware of teammates and defenders.

Protection in Traffic   There is often significant traffic inside the 8-meter area because this is the critical scoring area, and the defense will collapse into it. When a player feels the defense collapse, it is essential for her to protect her stick. Follow these five keys for stick protection in traffic:

- Choke up on the bottom hand. This allows for increased control and enables your body to protect the stick.
- Move the stick with small, quick cradles. The stick should not be away from your body and unprotected.
- Move the stick around quickly to avoid collapsing defenders.
- Be strong when cradling inside the 8-meter area.
- Keep your feet moving. If your feet stop moving, you will get checked. If you keep your feet moving, you can run out of trouble and are more likely to get fouled.

With regard to stickwork, note that there are a variety of stick positions for different players. Players will look different as they execute stickwork. Natural characteristics, like height, can significantly affect the way a player executes her stickwork. Each player must acknowledge her attributes and adjust her stickwork accordingly.

Deception

Deception is one of the most fundamental components for any successful lacrosse player. Deception is the appearance of one action and the execution of another. If a player is able to execute her passes, shots, and dodges without telegraphing their direction or timing, she will have a significant advantage over her opponent. A player has the ultimate awareness of what she plans to do next; if she is able to take an action without letting an opponent know what is to come, she has the advantage of timing on her side. The player will be a split second ahead of her opponent, who will be forced to react. Players need to use deception in practice and at full speed so they are confident enough to use deception in game situations. To be truly deceptive in using fakes, a player must mimic her normal shooting and passing body movements—and then do something different.

For a player to fake with her body, she shifts her weight from the back to front foot, squares her shoulders toward the target, and drives the elbow forward while keeping the head of the stick back. The stick should remain relatively still and in the triple-threat position, ready to pass or shoot after the fake. A body fake is designed to mimic the movement used in shooting and passing. Body fakes allow a player to remain a constant threat because an opponent will be unsure whether a shot or pass is coming.

Many types of stick fakes can be effective. For example, a player can fake the shot high, bring the stick across her body, and take an offside, low shot. A player can also fake a shot, switch hands as she pivots to the opposite side of the defender, and make a pass or a shot. These are two examples of the many stick fakes that use deception.

When faking, the player should keep her stick relatively quiet, with small cradles, so that she can pass or shoot at any point. Keep it simple. Use one fake and then shoot. One small movement is all it takes to get the goalie off balance.

Developing Offensive Skills

The most effective team offense is made up of individuals who have solid attacking skills: the ability to make basic attacking moves, get out of defensive pressure, and pass. If an individual player is able to be an offensive threat, she will increase opportunities for her teammates and make a valuable contribution to the team offense. This chapter details various individual attacking skills as they relate to a team offense.

Basic Attacking Moves

Attacking moves are what a player uses in beating a defender. However, it is not necessary for players to know and master every attacking move in existence to be a great attacker. Instead, players should learn and master one or two moves. A player who is able to consistently execute a couple of moves will be very successful. No one move is better than another—it is more about a player's ability to master a given move. The three keys to attacking moves are to make the move early, change speed, and change direction. The five basic attacking moves are split dodge, face dodge or stutter step, roll dodge, rocker dodge, and the question mark dodge.

Split Dodge

The split dodge focuses on change of direction, right to left or left to right. The split dodge is a simple move to learn and does not require sophisticated footwork. It does require switching hands, and the player needs to be comfortable with both hands before choosing a split dodge. With enough speed, the dodge can be effective; it is particularly useful when an attacker has significant time and space between herself and the defender. The split dodge is broken down into the following steps:

1. Run straight at the defender (figure 3.1a). Avoid veering off to the left or right because this will allow the defender to step up and slow the attacker down.

2. When approximately a stick's length away from the defender, start the move by faking in one direction (right or left).

3. To fake to the right, turn your shoulders slightly to the right and drive your shoulders in that direction (figure 3.1b). Then plant with the right (outside) foot.

4. When the defender commits to your right side, pull your stick across the body, switching hands (figure 3.1c).

5. Push off the right (planted) foot and accelerate past the defender (figure 3.1, d-f).

6. After beating the defender, cut her off by stepping in front of her (figure 3.1g). Do not veer off to one side. Protect your stick by keeping it in front and low, between your shoulders.

Note: To fake to the left, reverse steps 3 through 5.

 TIP If you are a right-handed player, consider faking to your left so you end up with the stick in your right (dominant) hand. Eventually, master this move with both hands.

(continued)

FIGURE 3.1 Split dodge.

FIGURE 3.1 *(continued)*

Face Dodge or Stutter Step

The face dodge is a good first dodge for a player to master. The footwork of the face dodge is very similar to that of the split dodge, but the face dodge does not require a player to switch hands. Following are the steps for a right-handed player.

1. Run straight at the defender (figure 3.2*a*).
2. When the player is approximately a stick's length away, pull your stick across your face to the left side of your body as if to beat the defender toward the left side (figure 3.2*b*). Make sure the stick is well protected and not hanging out in front.
3. Turn your shoulders slightly to the left, drive your left shoulder in that direction, and plant with the left (outside) foot.
4. When the defender commits, pull your stick back across your body and accelerate past the defender on the right side (figure 3.2*c*).
5. After beating your defender, cut her off by stepping in front of her (figure 3.2*d*). Do not veer off to one side. Protect your stick by keeping it in front, between your shoulders.

Note: Left-handed players should reverse steps 2 through 4.

FIGURE 3.2 Face dodge or stutter step.

Roll Dodge

The roll dodge is a relatively difficult move because the footwork can be complicated to learn and master. The roll dodge is effective when a defender pressures an attacker hard to one side or the other. The dodge allows the attacker to take advantage of the defender's commitment to one side. If you are right-handed, follow these steps:

1. Run straight at the defender (figure 3.3a).

2. As with the split dodge, turn your shoulders slightly to the right and drive your right shoulder in that direction. The objective is to get the defender to overcommit to your right side.

3. When the defender begins to commit, plant with your left (inside) foot on the defender's right side (figure 3.3b).

4. Turn your back to the defender and step across the defender's body with your right foot (figure 3.3c). Keep your stick between your shoulders to prevent the defender from getting a checkoff.

5. Step forward with your left foot to move around the defender (figure 3.3d). Come right off the defender's right shoulder, cutting her off, to prevent her from recovering back in front. Protect your stick by keeping it in front and low, between your shoulders.

Note: Left-handed players should reverse steps 2 through 5.

FIGURE 3.3 Roll dodge.

Rocker Dodge

The rocker dodge is an addendum to the roll dodge. This is also a fairly complicated move because it uses the same footwork as the roll dodge and adds an extra deceptive element. For a player who tends to use a roll dodge, the rocker dodge can be effective in catching a defender off balance. Follow these steps if you are right-handed:

1. Run straight at the defender (figure 3.4*a*).
2. Turn your shoulders slightly to the right and drive your right shoulder in that direction, similar to the move in the roll dodge. Plant with the left (inside) foot on the right side of the defender's body (figure 3.4*b*).
3. Turn your back to the defender and step across the defender's body with your right foot. Drive your right shoulder back and your left shoulder forward as if to continue the roll (figure 3.4, *c-d*). Keep your stick between the shoulders to prevent the defender from getting a checkoff.
4. When the defender commits to the roll, push off on your right foot, shift your weight onto your left foot, and step forward around the defender with your right foot (figure 3.4, *e-f*).
5. Come off the defender's right shoulder, cutting her off, to prevent her from recovering back in front (figure 3.4*g*).

Note: Left-handed players should reverse steps 2 through 5.

(continued)

FIGURE 3.4   Rocker dodge.

FIGURE 3.4 *(continued)*

Question Mark Dodge

The question mark dodge is a more advanced dodge and is particularly helpful for attackers who play around the crease. This dodge requires an attacker to initially go to goal with her strong hand, but the roll (outlined below) ultimately forces the player to finish the move and take a quick shot with her weak hand—all with enough time, space, and angle to maintain quality. As the attacker, follow these steps if you come from behind the net right-handed:

1. Drive around the crease with speed, as if attempting to beat the defender over the top with your right hand (figure 3.5*a*).

2. Drive hard, dropping your left shoulder to make the defender believe that you want to beat her with your right hand. The defender will step up to the stick and try to force you back down (figure 3.5*b*).

3. The first portion of the move is complete when the defender has committed to stopping your right-handed roll and you have driven far enough away from the crease to allow enough room to take a good angle shot. When the defender commits, quickly plant off the left (inside) foot, roll back (see roll dodge technique), and switch the stick to your left hand for a quick shot (figure 3.5*c*).

4. Take a step or two after planting with your left foot to create space between you and the defender (figure 3.5*d*). This will allow you enough space to take the shot.

Note: To roll from behind the net left-handed, reverse steps 1 through 4.

FIGURE 3.5 Question mark dodge.

Making a Move

Most people consider attack to be a finesse position. This is true in part: The attack position certainly requires and rewards stick skills. However, players need to avoid excessive fanciness when making an attacking move. There are three keys to an effective attacking move.

Speed   Speed is the key to an attacker's ability to beat a defender. The attacker must keep her feet moving throughout the entire move. When an attacker goes to goal, she must go hard. An attacking move at half speed will not be effective. Speed is especially effective when an attacker goes to goal from the midfield and from the top of the 8-meter area.

Space   Attackers should make their moves earlier than they might think is necessary. Moves should be made approximately a full stick's length away from a defender. If an attacker waits too long to initiate her move, she will eliminate the space needed to execute the move properly. This will also give a defender the opportunity to make a stick check because the attacker may bring her stick into the defender as she makes the move. Attackers must give themselves space to execute.

Time   With increased space comes increased time to execute a move. Neither dodges nor shots should be forced. When an attacker has the ball, she should have control over her situation and take her time. If there is no opening, the attacker should pull out and move the ball to another player, or reattack if a space opens.

Getting Out of Pressure

When a player goes 1v1 and reaches the 8-meter area, she often runs into a lot of pressure from the opposing defense. It is essential that players are able to stay composed and run out of pressure. The following keys will help a player handle pressure.

Anticipate   A player should anticipate when a defender will slide to her. Anticipation allows an extra second before she is doubled to make a move out of pressure.

Turn and Run Out of Pressure   Running is the fastest and most effective way to get out of pressure. Players should not shuffle backward; they should turn their feet and run in the opposite direction of the pressure.

Keep the Feet Moving   More often than not, a player stops moving her feet when she run into pressure. As soon as a player stops her feet, she has given the defenders a significant advantage. When a player is under intense pressure, it is essential to keep her feet moving.

Keep the Head Up   Even when a player is in the midst of running away from pressure, she must keep her head up and look for an open pass. Running out of pressure will allow the player time to regroup, but it is often best to move the ball to a teammate and force the defense to reset.

Don't Force It   When under pressure, it is important to stay composed and avoid rushing a pass or a shot. If the player does not see an available opening, she should run away from the pressure and look for a teammate to pop out and help. The first pass is not always the best one.

Passing Effectively

Making an effective pass is one of the most difficult skills and concepts in lacrosse. If a player is able to pass effectively, it will be easier for her teammates to successfully receive passes. An effective passer positively contributes to a smooth and well-connected unit. The following keys are components to a player's ability to pass effectively.

Be a Threat   A player needs to be a threat on the field in any given situation: 1v1 attempts, off-ball movement, passing, and so on. Even if a player intends to pass the ball, she still needs to appear as a threat to go to goal or to shoot. An attacker who routinely threatens to go to goal will keep the defense honest: The defense will be forced to pay constant attention to the ball carrier; consequently, other parts of the field, namely the middle, will open up for cutters.

Keep the Feet Moving   When an attacker stops her feet, she is no longer a threat on attack. When an attacker stands still, it becomes quite obvious to the defense that she plans to pass rather than go to goal. The defense will anticipate a pass and have a significantly better opportunity to knock down the ball or force a turnover.

Throw a Fake   Just as with shooting, when an attacker throws a fake before she makes a pass, it helps to throw the defender off. Being deceptive creates the time and space required for an effective pass. When a defense plays well and marks cutters tightly, even a small fake will help force the defense off balance and open up the offensive zone. An off-balance defense will often allow a pass to slip into the middle.

Developing Defensive Skills

The effectiveness of a defense is in the ability of the unit to work together. If any defender does not execute properly, it is difficult for the unit to function. If an individual defender is able to maintain her stick and body position, play body defense, force an attacker in a certain direction, and communicate with and slide to help fellow defenders, that defender will make a valuable contribution to their team. This chapter details various individual defensive skills as they relate to a team defense.

Stick and Body Positioning

Proper body positioning is one of the most fundamental characteristics of a great defender. Proper positioning allows for good body defense, clean checks, and forced turnovers. Defenders must always maintain an athletic body position. The defender's legs should be shoulder-width apart and knees should be bent (figure 4.1, *a-b*). The defender needs to be light on her feet and ready to move in any direction. Her weight should be on the balls of her feet, not the heels, to create good balance. The defender's upper body should be "big": arms away from the body and stick up in the air. The defender should maximize the surface area of her body. Defenders should not minimize their presence by shrinking down or bending over. Physical, verbal, and nonverbal cues announce her confident presence to the attacker.

The defender's stick should be almost vertical when she plays against an attacker. If the defender holds her stick straight up, she will have a better chance of knocking a ball down or getting a checkoff. A defender is also much less likely to have a foul called against her if her stick is in the vertical position.

FIGURE 4.1   Defensive body position.

Body Defense

A defender's focus should be on playing solid body defense: Focus on the opposing attacker and maintain body position in front of her. One of the best ways for a defender to play good body defense is to watch the attacker's hips. Unlike the attacker's eyes, stick, head, or shoulders, her hips do not lie. An attacker can use deception with her eyes, stick, and shoulders, but the hips generally give a very good indication of her movement. Defenders must be light on their feet, ready to react to the attackers' movements, and able to move side to side quickly. A defender can be effective if she watches the attacker's hips and is able to beat the attacker to the spot where she is going.

Part of good body defense is an ability to keep the attacker contained by maintaining control. Instead of being reactive, the defender should force the attacker to go to one side by taking away the space where the attacker wants to move (see Forcing on page 48). The defender should be physical and quick on her feet.

Checking

In women's lacrosse, a defender is allowed to use her stick to hit the attacker's stick in an attempt to knock the ball out. The check must be away from the attacker's body, in a downward direction, and must be a quick tap of the stick and a retreat back; the check cannot hold the attacker's stick down (figure 4.2, *a-c*).

Checking can be a supplement to solid body defense but not an alternative. If an attacker does not properly protect her stick, the defender may be able to quickly check the attacker's stick without compromising body positioning. Checks should be quick and executed only with the arms and stick, not the entire body. The defender should only go for a check in an opportune situation and should avoid wild checks. When a defender has good body defense, it is not necessary to worry about checking. Good body defense will force the attacker to make mistakes and turn over the ball on her own. With good body defense, checks will come naturally as they are needed. It is certainly acceptable for a defender to check sometimes, but she must never sacrifice body positioning for a check.

FIGURE 4.2   Checking.

Forcing

Defense is a team game. When a defender is 1v1 with an attacker, the ultimate goal is to force the attacker toward the defender's teammates. To force to help occurs when a defender positions her body so that she takes away space and directs an attacker toward her defensive teammates without allowing the attacker to move where she would like. To do so, the defender must step up to the opposite side of the direction she wants to attacker to go.

When a defender steps up to one side of an attacker, she uses her body as a road block. The goal is for the defender to position her body and stick so that the attacker cannot go around them in a particular direction. For example, if the defender chooses to step up to the attacker's right side, she will position her hips to be square with the attacker, with her left foot forward and in an athletic body position. The defender's body position should say to the attacker, "You cannot come in this direction." The defender must be strong in her stance to force the attacker in the designated (opposite) direction; the defender must also be light on her feet, with her weight on the balls of her feet (never on the heels), and able to move quickly. Because the defender has chosen to step up to the attacker's right side, the attacker will naturally try to go around the defender from the other side, in this case to the attacker's left side. It is acceptable for the attacker to beat the defender toward the side where she has been forced, in this case to the left side. In this situation, a supporting defender will be there to help (described in detail in the Sliding section on page 52).

The defender, however, must try not to overcommit to any one side. For example, if the defender chooses to force the attacker toward the attacker's left, the defender should not commit so far to the attacker's right side that the defender is unable to adjust and maintain body position. If the attacker is able to easily beat the defender toward that left side, the defensive player will have been removed from the play, and the attacker will be free to continue her threat. Forcing is a proactive defensive position to limit the attacker's option to one direction and slow down the attacker's forward movement. The defensive goal is to contain the attacker, slow her down, maintain body position, and prevent an uncontested path to the goal.

The defender's job is not finished even if she has forced the attacker to help. After a defender has forced an attacker to her weak hand or into defensive pressure, the defender must anticipate that the attacker will roll back, either to her strong hand or away from pressure. The defender should be prepared for the attacker to try to roll out of the pressure and must force her back to the defensive help again and again.

It can seem risky for a defender to step up and force an attacker in one direction, because the defender essentially gives the attacker space to beat her toward that side. This is why the defender's teammates need to be ready to slide early. Communication is one of the most critical elements in a defender's ability to force an attacker to help. The defender who is adjacent to the ball—and defending the attacker who is directly next to the attacker with the ball—is primarily responsible for communicating where she is and where the on-ball defender should force the attacker. Even so, every player on the field carries this responsibility and should be aware of which way a defender should force. The direction to force must be constantly communicated among the members of a defensive unit. Communication becomes vital if an attacking team sets up an isolation, which is when they clear one side of the 8-meter area to allow an attacker to go 1v1. In this situation, every defensive player who sees the isolation must communicate to the on-ball defender where her help is. The following are examples of communicative commands.

Force Left or Force Right   The direction called out, left or right, refers to that of the defender and goaltender looking upfield. To force right is to force an attacker to the defender's right side and to the attacker's left hand (figure 4.3, *a-b*). To force an attacker left is to force her to the defender's left side and to the attacker's right hand (figure 4.4, *a-b*).

FIGURE 4.3   Forcing right.

FIGURE 4.4 Forcing left.

Force Back A defender should call out "Force left" or "Force right" unless she is in a clear double-team situation, when calling out "Force back" can be helpful. In this case, a call to force back implies that a supporting defender will direct the on-ball defender to step up to the attacker and force her in the opposite direction, back toward the support.

Defenders often choose to force an attacker to the attacker's weak hand. This can be effective if the attacker is not particularly skilled with her weak hand. However, if the defender does not have help in the weak-hand direction, she should force the attacker to help, rather than toward the attacker's weak hand.

Sliding

A defense must work together as a unit. When one defender gets beaten by an attacker, her teammates must be there to back her up. Sliding is the technical name for backing up a teammate; the term is used to represent the movement of a defender from her current position so she can help a fellow defender.

Sliding is one of the most critical defensive skills because it prevents a defense from collapsing after one defender has been beaten by an attacker. For example, if a defender gets beaten and no one slides to help, the attacker is free to go to goal uncontested. On the other hand, if one defender gets beaten and another slides to help, this allows the first defender to recover body position and either pick up the original attacker or fill in for the defender who has just slid to back them up. Getting beaten as a defender is not the end of the world—as long as the defender communicates with a fellow defender to slide to help.

The term *first slide* refers to the defender directly next to the ball (right or left side) who slides to help the on-ball defender. The term *second slide* refers to the defender directly next to the first slide who slides to cover the attacker left open by the first slide. Numerous slides often occur until the ball carrier is contained, and the defense is able to reset into man-to-man coverage. Following are a few basic keys to sliding.

Anticipate One of the most vital parts of good team defense is anticipation of the need to slide. It may seem strange, but a defender should expect a teammate to get beaten. If a defender does so, she will always be ready and in position to make a slide to help when necessary (figure 4.5, *a-b*).

Slide With the Body When a defender slides, she should slide with her body, not her stick. A slide typically comes because a teammate has been beaten (figure 4.5*c*). The supporting defender must focus on slowing the attacker down by using her body. The supporting defender cannot afford to go for a check and get beaten, too.

Slide Hard The defender must slide hard and with a purpose; she cannot be scared or reluctant (figure 4.5*d*). A half-hearted slide can be more detrimental than no slide at all. A purposeful slide will surprise the attacker and will also help fellow defenders make the second and third slides effectively.

Communicate the Slide If a defender communicates when she slides and where she slides from, she can do no wrong. The

FIGURE 4.5 Sliding to help.

defender cannot assume that her teammates can read her mind or see her slide. The sliding defender must communicate to the rest of the defense so that they know who will be left open after the slide, and where they need to slide next.

Get Back After a defender makes a slide and the attacker moves the ball or backs out of pressure, the defender must hustle to find the open attacker. When the defender slid, she was forced to leave her original attacker behind. Another defender likely made the second slide to back up the defender who had slid first, thus leaving another attacker open. When a defender slides to an attacker, it is because that attacker is an immediate threat. When the threat lessens, the defender should back off and rebalance the defense by finding and defending against an open attacker.

Communicate the Open Player It is just as essential to communicate after a slide as it is to communicate before. When a defender or a supporting defender stops the ball, she must get back into the team's settled defense. The entire defense must communicate where the open player is so that the sliding defender can get matched up as quickly as possible.

Anticipate Angles Angles determine the effectiveness of sliding. Players should anticipate where the attacker will be and slide to that spot rather than slide to where the attacker was.

The Double-Team

When a defender forces an attacker to help, the defender creates a double-team situation. With patience and smart execution, defenders using a double-team can cause an attacker to turn the ball over or make a bad decision. Positioning and communication are the keys to an effective double-team.

When a double-team is formed between two defenders, they must position themselves so that they do not cut each other off. One defender should cover the attacker's stick, and the other defender should cover the attacker's body. The defenders must communicate who will cover what. Both defenders should position themselves very close to the attacker's body to form a V shape and force the attacker to attempt to go between the two defenders as the only option (figure 4.6).

If the attacker tries to go to the outside of one of the defenders, that defender must force the attacker back to the other defender,

FIGURE 4.6 Double-team positioning.

just as in a settled 1v1 situation (i.e., step up to her side; figure 4.7, *a-c*). If the attacker tries to go through the middle of the two defenders, the defenders simply need to close the gap with their bodies (figure 4.8, *a-b*). Defenders may be tempted to go for a check, but checks are risky. The defenders should first establish solid body position by closing the gap with their bodies; the check will come next. The defenders must be prepared for the roll back in a double-team situation. The attacker will always try to get out of pressure, usually by rolling in the opposite direction. The defenders should anticipate and be ready for the roll back.

After the initial slide to double an attacker, the supporting defender can choose to stay on the double-team or return to defend against her original player. If both defenders choose to stay on the double, they must communicate with each other and continue to pressure the attacker so that it's difficult for her to find the open player and make a pass out of pressure. A defender should stay on the double if

- the defenders are able to maintain good pressure on the attacker after the initial slide,
- the defenders can feel the attacker getting flustered,
- the attacker is one of the team's weaker players, or
- the defenders do not think the attacker will be able to pass or make a good decision under pressure.

FIGURE 4.7 Double-team movement: Attacker tries to go outside of defender.

FIGURE 4.8 Double-team movement: Attacker tries to go through defenders.

In certain situations, after the initial slide to double, it is better for the defender to back off and return to the open attacker. The decision to stay on or drop off the double depends on the defensive scheme, the opposing team, or the time remaining in the game. A defender should drop off the double if

- the defenders are not able to establish good pressure on the attacker,
- the defenders feel vulnerable to getting beaten,
- the attacker anticipates the pressure and backs out before the defense can form a solid double-team, or
- the defensive scheme is not high pressure or high risk.

If a defender drops off the double-team, she must quickly find the open player. However, the defender must not leave the double blindly. A good, aggressive attacker is likely to feel the pressure release and try to reattack. The supporting defender should find the open player without taking her eyes off the ball.

After the attacker passes out of the double-team, both defenders should fall back into the defense. The defenders should communicate with and listen to their fellow defenders to quickly find the open player and balance the defense.

Communication in a double-team situation is essential. Communication does not become any less important when there are two defenders against one attacker. The defenders must communicate who has body, who has stick, and where to force. Following are a few communicative commands.

I've Got Body   When a defender calls out, "I've got body," it means the defender is focused on playing solid body defense. The body defender will not go for a check; she is simply working to contain and slow the attacker with her body.

I've Got Stick   When a defender calls out, "I've got stick," it means this defender is in a better position to make a check. She must still play body defense, but the defender on the stick is aggressive and looking for a check.

Force Back   A call of "Force back" is used by a defender to indicate to a teammate that she needs to step up and force the attacker in the opposite direction, toward the communicating defender.

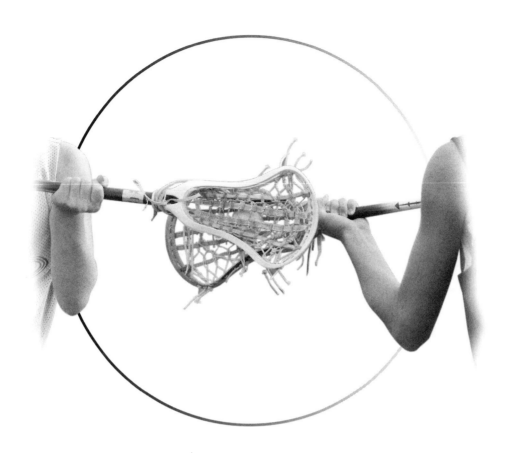

PART II
Team Play

Team Attacking

The key to an effective attacking unit is the ability to combine individual attacking skills into a cohesive unit that operates according to certain attacking concepts. Because every movement made by an attacker will affect the other six attackers in the unit, each movement must be coordinated. An attack must constantly move around the zone, move the ball, and use space to develop offensive opportunities. This chapter details various attacking concepts related to a full offensive unit of seven players.

Basic Attacking Movement

To create scoring opportunities, an attacking unit needs to capitalize on their possession of the ball. The attacking players must constantly move themselves and the ball around the zone, forcing the defense to react to their movement. As discussed later, the goal is to maximize the space in the zone, create space for scoring opportunities, and do so with speed and coordinated timing.

Composure and confidence are two fundamental characteristics of a successful attack. Throughout the course of a game and certainly a season, a team will face many defenses: high pressure, low pressure, or even a zone. For a team to be successful, it is essential for all players to stay composed, maintain control, and play their game regardless of the defense faced. A successful team does not get flustered; team members recognize the given defense, adapt to it, and make smart decisions.

As outlined in chapter 3, the keys to attack are speed, space, and time. The same keys apply to a team's attacking motion. Timing becomes increasingly important because seven players, rather than one, are now involved. The principles of running an attacking motion are covered in the following sections.

Positioning

There are no concrete rules that govern an attacking setup. However, one or two players must be behind the net at all times. If a shot goes wide of the net, someone needs to be behind the net to back it up. Aside from the player or players behind the net, the remaining players must stay big (spread out, outside the 12-meter area) to allow adequate space to set up and execute attacking plays. When an attack stays small (sucked into the 8-meter area), it is more difficult to drive 1v1 or find open cutters in the middle. A small attack also makes it easier for the defense to slide and cover cutters.

1v1

The 1v1 is one of the most effective ways to create a good scoring opportunity. For the 1v1 to be successful, the rest of the attack must first clear space for the 1v1 attacker. Space can be created by clearing through for the attacker going 1v1, allowing the attacker open space toward her dominant side. The two attackers closest to the ball on the strong side should cut through to the opposite side of the 8-meter area. This clearing movement will remove the remaining attackers and the opposing defenders from the 1v1 attacker's way. If the attacker is right-handed, players will clear the right side; if she is left-handed, players will clear the left side. Note that even though the supporting attackers are cutting to create space for their teammate to go to goal, they should be prepared to receive the ball and remain a threat so that the defense continues to follow them.

After the space has opened up, the 1v1 attacker should challenge her defender and take the ball to goal. To execute a 1v1, follow these guidelines:

- Be patient. Do not get too anxious and rush the 1v1 before the space has cleared. Wait for the supporting attackers to cut through and then make a move into the open space.
- Go hard. Speed kills. After taking the open space, commit to it and go hard to goal. Not only is speed important, but change of speed is as well.
- Don't force it. If you do not have a good scoring opportunity, do not force a shot. Pull out of the pressure and get ready to reattack or make a pass.

Ball Movement

Moving the ball from player to player around the offensive zone is one of the most effective ways to get the defense off balance and create openings for the attack. As the ball is passed around between the attacking players, the defense is forced to shift and adjust to each position of the ball, making it difficult for them to get comfortable.

Sometimes the 1v1 does not open up as planned. When the 1v1 is not open, it should not be forced. Instead, the 1v1 attacker should use outlets—passing options—for the ball. The two attackers on either side of the ball carrier should pop out, or break away from their defenders and from pressure so that they can be supporting outlets for the player who has decided not to go 1v1 and seeks an outlet to pass the ball.

When an attacker passes out of pressure to an outlet, it is important for the attack to move the ball one more time. One outlet pass is not sufficient because it does not force the defensive players to readjust their positions. A second pass will switch the attacking point to the weak side, force the defense to shift, and expose any openings in the defense. It is crucial to move the ball twice to the weak side.

After the ball has moved to the other side of the field, it is time to reattack. The attack can try to go 1v1 again (from a different vantage point and perhaps with a different player) or look for the open pass in the middle (only if it is clearly open). As the defense shifts to get back into position, there will be many openings and potential to attack.

Off-Ball Movement

The 1v1s and ball movement are fundamental elements to the attack's basic motion, but an attack cannot be successful without effective off-ball movement. Off-ball movement refers to the movement of the six attacking players who do not possess the ball. When one attacking player has the ball, the remaining six players who do not have the ball must keep their defenders occupied. They must make it more difficult for defenders to focus on the ball carrier, see open cutters, or make necessary slides. There are several options for off-ball movement: picks, the exchange of field positions with teammates, and fake cuts. Off-ball players need to be aware of the ball carrier and her space at all times. Off-ball players should not cut into the ball carrier's space and must recognize when the ball carrier needs to make a supporting pass.

Figure 5.1 illustrates a basic attacking motion, including a balanced setup (5.1a); off-ball movement to create space (5.1, b-c); a 1v1 attack (5.1d); and the decision to pull out (5.1e), opt for an outlet pass (5.1f), and reset the balanced setup for a reattack (5.1, g-h). These same motions apply if the outlet pass is made to the player behind the net instead of to the player up top (player 6 rather than player 1 in 5.1f).

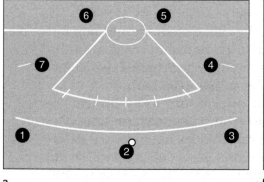 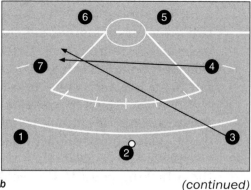

a b (continued)

FIGURE 5.1 Breaking down the attack: (a) basic, balanced attacking setup; (b) two players closest to the ball (3 and 4; strong side) cut through.

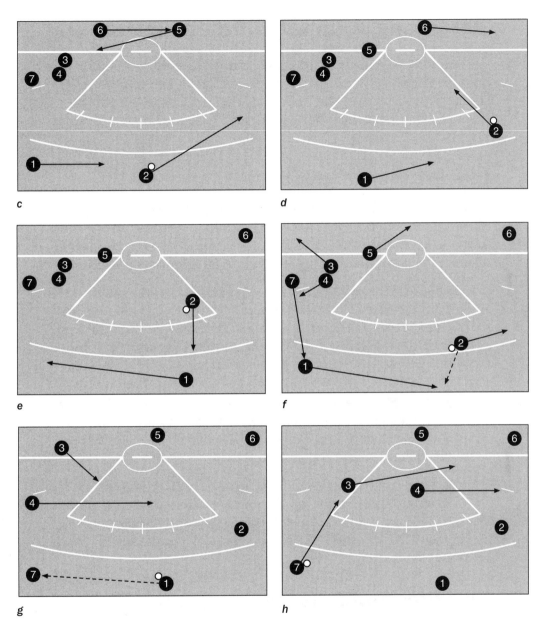

FIGURE 5.1 Breaking down the attack *(continued)*: *(c)* the low attacker, player 5, cuts to the other side to open a space; *(d)* player 2 takes 1v1 and adjacent players (1 and 6) start to drift toward the ball as outlets; *(e)* player 2 pulls out if no 1v1 and adjacent player (1) pops out as a supporting outlet; *(f)* offense stays big and player 2 moves the ball to the adjacent outlet (1); *(g)* attack moves the ball again and clears space for a new 1v1; *(h)* attackers attack other side with 1v1.

Attacking Against Different Defenses

Throughout a season, a team will undoubtedly face different defenses from different opponents. A team must be able to remain in control and play their game regardless of the opposing defense. There are various ways to face low- and high-pressure defenses.

Low-Pressure Defense

If the defense backs off their opposing attackers and sags into the 8-meter area, they have allowed the attack both time and space. As outlined earlier, time and space are two keys to a successful attack. The attack can take advantage by following these keys:

- The attack should stay big, spread out, and outside the 12-meter area. In a low-pressure scenario, the defense has chosen to give the attack space. It behooves the attack to take it and use it to their advantage. The attack should not get sucked into the 8-meter area.

- The attack should follow a basic attacking motion: clear space, take the 1v1, and move the ball. The 1v1 will be even more effective when an attacker is given the space to gain speed and momentum as she carries the ball toward her defender and toward the goal.

With good ball movement, the attack will create effective 1v1s, draw double-teams, and force the defense to shift often. The attack may even catch the defense in the shooting space as they shift. The attack must be aggressive with the 1v1 and off-ball movement.

High-Pressure Defense

If the defense pressures the attackers out, the defense is vulnerable to get beaten 1v1. The attacker must handle the pressure, stay composed, and attempt to beat her defender 1v1. Once the attacker beats her defender, she must continue to move her feet and protect her stick by bringing it in front of her body and between her shoulders. The defense will not give up; they will look for opportunities to check from behind.

After the attacker beats the defender 1v1, she must anticipate that a supporting defender will slide to her and leave someone open. The ball-carrying attacker must have her head up and make a pass to the open attacker. If the defender fails to slide in time, the attacker should continue the 1v1 move to goal.

The keys to a team's success against a high-pressure defense are to maintain their game and avoid getting flustered. Players must be composed and have confidence in their stick skills and ability to beat a defender 1v1. After a player beats her defender 1v1, she must be aware of and able to find the openings.

 TIP Some high-pressure defenses do not pressure attackers behind the net. In this case, the area behind the net acts as a safe zone, a place to set up the attack and calm everyone down. If the defense does pressure behind the goal, the attack should challenge any defenders and take them to goal.

Cutting

Cutting refers to the off-ball movement of an attacker from one position in the offensive zone to another. Most often, a cut is directly through the 8-meter scoring area and is designed to open up the cutting player to receive the ball, to force the defender to chase the cutter, and to create space for other attacking players. A cut must be at full speed and timed correctly. In addition, the cutter must be ready to receive the ball. Cutters can create a lot of opportunities, not only for themselves, but for their teammates. Cutters create space, which is one of the fundamental keys to a team attack. Following are characteristics of a good cutter.

Always Be a Threat   When an attacker makes a cut, even if simply clearing space for a teammate, she must always be ready to receive the ball. This will force the defense to play honestly and make their decisions much more difficult: Should they follow the cutter through her cut or slide to the ball? If both the cutter and the ball carrier are threats, the defense will be forced to choose between the two. And even if the attacker's intent is just to clear space, the situation may end up with the cutter wide open to receive a pass.

Finish the Cut   The cutting attacker must cut all the way through the 8-meter area. An attacker may be tempted to stop in the middle of the 8-meter area, halfway through her cut. This clogs up the middle for other attackers who may be open. To prevent clogging up the middle, the attacker must finish her cut.

Have Good Timing Timing plays a crucial role in an attacker's ability to make a cut. An attacker must be aware of her teammates before she makes a cut to avoid moving into a teammate's space. The attacker should also watch her defender: If the defender looks away and the back of her head becomes visible—even for a split second—that is a good time to catch her off guard and cut. If an attacker is next to a ball carrier who is looking to go 1v1, the cutter should immediately cut through to open up space.

Use Both Hands An attacker needs to be able to cut and catch with both hands. If an attacker can cut both right- and left-handed, she becomes a much bigger threat: There will be more openings in the 8-meter area for her and more scoring chances. If an attacker gets ahead of her defender on a cut, and the ball is passed to her, the attacker needs to make the catch between her shoulders and use her body to protect her stick from a trailing defender who will look for back checks.

Offensive Communication

Communication is most often discussed on defense but rarely addressed for the offensive end of the field. Communication is as important on attack as it is on defense. For an attack to flow smoothly and be executed successfully, all attacking players need to be on the same page. The importance of timing has been stressed throughout this chapter, and communication facilitates quality timing. Sometimes a simple head nod or a few words can be the defining variable between a successful and an unsuccessful attack.

Many attack situations call for communication. If a player wants to take the ball 1v1, she should let her teammates know to cut through to create space. If a player realizes that her teammate with the ball has a good 1v1 opportunity, she should encourage the ball carrier to take the 1v1 and direct other teammates to create space. If the ball carrier is unable to convert the 1v1, the outlet players must let everyone know they are open for a supporting pass. If the attack runs a specific play, the players should direct each other where to go. Communication should be clear and directive. It is difficult to find any attacking scenario that does not require communication between the attacking players.

SUMMARY: Six Keys to Team Attacking

Stay big: When an attack stays big, the attacking players will create time and space. Attackers should stay outside the 12-meter area unless they are cutting through the 8.

Move off the ball: If attacking players without the ball move continuously, the defenders will be forced to attend to both the ball carrier and the cutters. When the defenders pay attention to cutters, they create openings for the 1v1. Off-ball movement is a way to open up space.

Be a threat: Attackers must be threats wherever they are on the field. If an attacker has the ball, she should aggressively attack the goal and force the defense to slide and play her. If an attacker is off the ball, she should make hard cuts and ask for the ball.

Don't force it: Attackers must find the balance between being aggressive and being smart. Sometimes the best decision is to pull out and pass. It is essential to be a threat first and then back out if the opportunity is not there. Attackers must take their time, continue to challenge the defense, and wait for the best opportunity.

Move the ball: The attack should constantly move the ball around the offensive zone and attack from different points on the field: right side, left side, up top, and behind. Attacking movement forces the defense to adjust and creates openings. Patient ball movement will create the best possible scoring chances.

Communicate: Communication is as important on attack as it is on defense. Communication allows attackers to work collectively as a unit. Communication should be consistent and directive. It is just as important to listen as it is to talk.

Team Defense

If a defensive unit is able to limit an opponent's scoring opportunities, they will put their team in a favorable position to win a game. As is the case with an attacking unit, defenders must work cohesively. Perhaps more so than with any other position on the field, any action or inaction by a defensive player will affect the overall success of the unit. Nearly any defensive action can be supported, adjusted to, or rectified by the rest of the unit if the action is communicated.

This chapter breaks down the basic man-to-man defense. This particular defense is referred to as match-up or man-to-man defense, but it is essential to remember that defense is a team game. Each defender must consider the various opponents around her and avoid focusing solely on one attacker. There are two ways to play man-to-man defense: high pressure and low pressure. The unique concepts and benefits of low- and high-pressure defenses are discussed in the following sections.

Low-Pressure Defense

A low-pressure defense is characterized by defenders who sag into the 8-meter area and wait for opposing attackers to come to them. As an attacker approaches the 12-meter area, the defender prepares to pick her up. When the attacker reaches the 8-meter area, the defender marks her. If the attacker pulls out of pressure and back outside the 12-meter area, the defender drops back to the 8-meter area.

In a low-pressure defense, the on-ball defender does not chase the attacker outside the 12-meter area; neither do the off-ball defenders. Off-ball defenders should sag into the 8-meter area and off their attackers to provide help when needed. When an attacker cuts through the 8-meter area, the defender then marks her tightly. When a defender marks a cutter through the 8-meter area, she must work to get in front of the attacker's stick. The attacker should not be able to cut easily through the 8-meter area with her strong hand.

There are several advantages to a low-pressure defense. It can help a team learn the basic concepts of team defense: helping, sliding, and communicating. It is easier for the defense to anticipate and execute defensive slides because everyone is compacted and settled into the confined 8-meter area. It limits the time attackers have to make decisions in the critical scoring area because the defense is so compact.

There are also several disadvantages to a low-pressure defense: It affords the attacking team significant time and space. Time and space are two keys to an attack, and as a general rule, the defense should work to take away time and space from an attack. A low-pressure defense is reactive rather than proactive. It allows an attacking team the time, space, and control to execute at their pace.

High-Pressure Defense

A high-pressure defense is characterized by constant pressure on the ball, wherever the attacker possesses it. A high-pressure defense is proactive and forces the attacker to make a decision she may not be ready to make. In a low-pressure defense, the attacker is able to stay outside the 12-meter area without being pressured by the defense until she is ready to make her move. With a high-pressure defense, however, defenders chase the attacker and pressure her regardless of her position in the attacking zone. The high-pressure defense maintains control by limiting the attacker's time and space to make a decision and execute.

When a defender pressures the ball, she becomes increasingly vulnerable to getting beaten 1v1. Supporting defenders must realize and anticipate that the on-ball defender may get beaten. Off-ball defenders must be ready to slide early. The key to a high-pressure defense is anticipating the need for an early slide by supporting defenders.

Supporting off-ball defenders must be on their toes, communicating and being ready to slide to help early. In a high-pressure defense, the off-ball defenders adjacent to the ball (to the left or right side) will be the first slide. These defenders must communicate constantly with the on-ball defender so everyone knows which way to force the attacker and where the help is.

There are several advantages to a high-pressure defense: It is proactive and puts pressure on the attack. When an attacker is pressured, she is forced to make decisions she may not be ready to make. High-pressure defense can limit the time and space needed for an attack to be executed.

There are also several disadvantages to a high-pressure defense: It is not ideal for a team that has not yet mastered the basic defensive concepts of helping, sliding, and communicating. High-pressure defense requires significant communication and hard work. In a high-pressure defense, defensive players must have good foot speed, commit to ball pressure, anticipate that the on-ball defender will get beaten, communicate, and slide to help early.

Figure 6.1 on page 75 shows the setup of a high-pressure defense; figure 6.2 on page 76 breaks down the high-pressure defense.

Defender 1 The on-ball defender puts as much pressure on the ball as possible (6.2a). This defender should be confident in stepping out and pressuring the ball. She needs to get to the attacker's stick and force the attacker to the direction of the help defender. The help defenders are key to the success of the high-pressure defense.

 TIP It is okay for the on-ball defender to get beaten when she pressures the ball. Players often hesitate to put a lot of pressure on the ball because they are afraid to get beaten. Defense is a team game, and defensive teammates will support the on-ball defender when she gets beaten. Ball pressure is the key to a high-pressure defense.

Defenders 2 and 7   The adjacent defenders are alert and ready to help. A slide from the adjacent defender (6.2*b*) will create a double-team on the ball. The goal is for the on-ball defender to force the attacker to the sliding defender. If it is decided that 7 will be the first slide, she must communicate with 1: "With you right," "Force right." Defender 7 is ready to slide but does not want to allow her attacker to be an easy outlet pass. Defender 7 must be very active and alert.

Defender 2 is the first slide if 7 is not in the position to make the initial slide. Otherwise, 2 can drop off her attacker slightly. She must be alert, aware of the 8-meter area, and ready to help with an attacker who is open on a cut. Defender 2 also must be aware of the ball carrier, maintain appropriate position, and anticipate a need to slide. If the ball carrier's back is turned away from 2, she can drop off her attacker and look to help in the middle. If the ball carrier is facing 2, the defender should be ready to slide or eliminate the easy outlet pass.

Defender 6   If 7 is the first slide, this defender is the second slide. She must communicate constantly with 7. It is 6's job to initiate the first slide by telling 7, "You can go." When 7 slides to the ball, 6 is responsible for picking up 7's player.

 TIP   Defenders are often reluctant to slide to the ball because they are nervous about leaving their players open. The second slide must initiate the first slide by reassuring her teammate that she will cover her player. Key phrases are "I'm with you," "You can go," and "Slide."

Defender 3   If 7 is the first slide, 3 can drop off her attacker and focus on helping in the middle with open attackers. After the first and second slides occur, there will be a lot of traffic in the 8-meter area.

Defenders 4 and 5   The low defenders are the anchors of the defense. These defenders can see the whole field and must communicate to their teammates when to slide and who is open. Low defenders are also responsible for marking open attackers in the middle. If a defender simply puts out her stick for a second on an open cutter, this can deter the cutter from receiving a pass. It is important for the low defenders not to get lazy. Low defenders must be as active and alert as everyone else on the field.

TIP The goalie should ultimately lead the defensive communication. From her vantage point, the goalie can see everything. She must be a loud, directive, and vocal leader on the field.

Figure 6.1 illustrates a high-pressure defensive setup and the role played by each defender. Figure 6.2 provides a step-by-step breakdown of a high-pressure defensive movement. The on-ball defender (defender 1) initiates the high pressure defense by putting as much pressure on the ball as possible and forcing the attacker to her weak side. In this diagram, the attacker is right-handed and the defender forces her to her left hand, or to the right side of the 8-meter area (6.2*a*). Remember, defensive directions are from the perspective of the goalkeeper. The adjacent defenders, defender 7 and defender 2, are ready to slide. In this case, defender 7 slides to the double-team because the attacker has been forced to the right side. Defender 7 slides early and hard to create a double-team on the ball with defender 1 (6.2*b*). Because defender 7 has made the first slide, defender 6 is now responsible for the second slide to cover the attacker left open by defender 7 (6.2*c*). If the double-team is effective, the attacker will be forced to pull out of the pressure and move the ball to her teammate, who cuts for an outlet pass (6.2, *d-e*). When the ball moves, in this case further to the right, defender 5 slides to ball and defender 4 shifts across the crease to become the adjacent defender (6.2*e*). Defender 1 must drop off the former double-team and back to the weak side to pick up the extra attacker who has been left open. While defender 1 is making this shift, the rest of the defense on the weak side remain in a zone defense because there are only three defenders to cover four attackers after defender 4 slides from the weak side to the on-ball's adjacent defender (6.2*f*). When defender 1 gets back into the weak side, the defense can reorganize into the high-pressure defensive setup (see figure 6.1) and prepare for another on-ball double-team (6.2*g*).

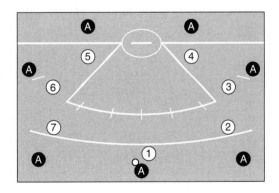

FIGURE 6.1 High-pressure defensive setup.

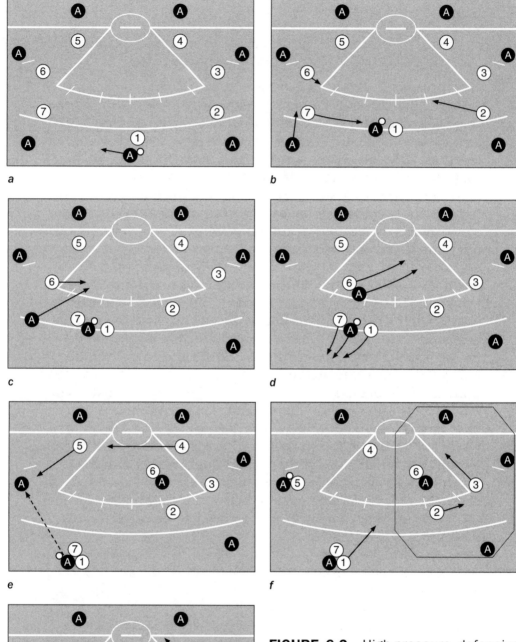

FIGURE 6.2 High-pressure defensive breakdown: *(a)* force the weak ball; *(b)* slide early and hard; *(c)* second slide for a double-team; *(d)* attacker pulls out and the defense is ready to shift; *(e)* the ball moves, and low defenders shift and slide up and across the crease; *(f)* zone weak side until 1 gets back; *(g)* defense is organized.

In a double-team, the stick-side defender should step up to the attacker's stick and force her back to her defensive teammate. Neither defender should overcommit. One player should play body, and the other can look for the check. Key words to use to communicate with other defenders include "I have body," "I have stick," and "Force her back."

Communication is the key to an effective double-team. A defender should communicate every time she slides. She must tell her teammates where she is leaving so the defense knows where the open attacker is. The defender cannot assume that her teammates will know when she plans to slide. High-pressure defense is hectic by definition, and communication is the key. Key phrases include "I'm leaving," "Watch low," and "Watch left, right, or middle" depending on the situation.

If the attacker pulls out of the double-team pressure, the defenders need to make a decision. The defense can either stay on the double or drop off and find the open attacker. If the defense has a strong double-team and can feel the attacker getting flustered, they should keep the pressure on. If not, the second defender should drop off, find an open attacker, and reset the defense.

If the defender drops off the double-team, she must be aware of the reattack. The defender should watch the ball as she drops off to find the open player. When the ball is moved, the defender should hustle back into the defense and get organized. The defense must always keep pressure on the ball and prevent the attacker from getting settled and finding the open pass.

 TIP The ball may move faster than shown in figure 6.2. The defense must stay calm, communicate about the open players, pressure the ball, and constantly check the middle of the 8-meter area for open players.

Both defenses make use of the same principles—ball pressure, slides, and defensive shifts—although there are significant differences. There is much less intense ball pressure in the low-pressure defense than in the high-pressure version. The low-pressure defense is more compact than the high-pressure defense because the defensive players do not allow themselves to get pulled out beyond the 12-meter area. As a result, the slides tend to be closer. There will not be as many defensive shifts in the low-pressure defense as in the high-pressure defense shown in figure 6.2. A low-pressure defense consists of short slides to ball and back to the attacker, whereas the high-pressure defense emphasizes constant pressure on the ball and the attacker.

Defensive Communication

Communication is the foundation of any good defense. Each player must talk and listen. A team should establish specific words or phrases that work for the team, a language that every player understands and responds to.

It is important to distinguish between scenarios that necessitate specific types of communication. Certain defensive situations call for routine communication, and others demand urgent action. Distinctions are made with changes in volume and tone of voice.

On-Ball Communication

"Got ball" signifies that a particular defender is guarding the attacker with the ball ("I got ball," "You got ball," "Ashley's got ball").

"Help!" is an urgent call used by a defender when she gets beaten—even by a step—and needs help.

Off-Ball Communication

"With you right" and "With you left" signify that a defender is ready to help the on-ball defender from a specific direction.

"Force right" or "Force left" is a command used by a defender or goalie to tell a teammate which way to force an attacker.

"Help!" is an urgent call signifying that a defender needs help with an open attacker.

"Middle!" is an urgent call signifying that an attacker is open in the middle.

"Watch low," "Watch high," "Watch right," and "Watch left" are used by a defender when she slides to help to alert her teammates that she has left an attacker open.

Defensive units find it helpful to develop a list of words with specific meanings. For example, a team may designate a specific phrase such as "I'm key" to signify to teammates that a defender is the first slide. This phrase can be used in conjunction with other defensive communication: "Force right, I'm key" or "I'm key, force right." Using words with specific meanings helps a defensive unit remain on the same page.

Communication must be repeated. It is loud on the field, and players can easily miss communication if it is not directive and repetitive. If a phrase is repeated, everyone will know who is sliding, and players can anticipate and adjust appropriately.

SUMMARY: Six Keys to Team Defense

Make it difficult for the attack: The defense should put pressure on the attackers and prevent them from controlling the pace. Take away time and space. Be physical.

Get to the stick: Defenders should get to the attacker's stick. This slows the attacker down because it forces her to make a move or change direction. Off-ball defenders should also get to the attacker's stick and prevent her from cutting through the 8-meter area with her strong hand open to receive a pass.

Slide early: Defenders should not hesitate to slide early. As a sliding defender, it is okay to cheat a little, to hedge toward the ball in anticipation. Anticipate and communicate. A defender cannot go wrong as long as she communicates.

Be aggressive: Defenders must commit to winning 50–50 balls. Back up the net. Pressure the attackers all over. The ultimate goal is to gain possession of the ball.

Play body: Defenders must play aggressive—but not reckless—body defense and never sacrifice defensive positioning for a check. Good body defense will force opponents to make mistakes.

Communicate: Communication cannot be emphasized enough. Defensive players must communicate everything so that their teammates can react to the attack and to defensive decisions. Every player on defense must constantly talk and listen. Defense is a team game, and communication allows a unit to work together. Communication is essential to defensive success.

Team Breaks and Transitions

During the course of a game, there will be numerous instances when ball possession switches from one team to another. When a team loses possession of the ball, it is referred to as a turnover. Turnovers occur when the goalie makes a save, an attacker drops the ball, a defender strips the ball from an attacker, or any situation occurs that results in a change of possession. When a change of possession happens, each team must make immediate shifts, both mentally and physically. The defense must shift into an offensive mode, and the offense must switch into a defensive mode. This chapter discusses the keys to offensive and defensive transitions.

Offensive Transitions

When a turnover occurs, the defense must immediately shift the ball and themselves out of their defensive zone into the midfield and ultimately into their offensive zone. The movement of the ball and the defensive players out of the defensive zone is referred to as a breakout, and the entire shift from defense to offense is referred to as a transition. A clear is a pass or series of passes that move the ball out of the defensive zone. A clear can begin with the goalie, or with any defensive player who possesses the ball at the point of turnover. If a team is able to clear the ball, break out of the defensive zone, and transition from defense to offense, they will create significant scoring opportunities. Scoring opportunities are often created in transition. The following sections outline keys to effective offensive transitions.

Clearing and breakout concepts are discussed in detail in chapter 8, but the general concepts of an offensive transition are as follows:

- When the defensive team gains possession of the ball, players should spread out immediately and make cuts for the ball.

- Breakouts should progress down the sides of the field rather than down the middle. This will maximize space by spreading players out across the field and avoid the danger that would occur if the ball was turned over in the middle of the field during the transition. If the opposing team is able to recover a turnover in the middle of the field, they will have a clearer path to the goal than if the ball is turned over along the side of the field.

- Generally speaking, after the ball is broken out, players should pass it behind the net to shift the play to the opposite side of the field. As the team that lost possession transitions into their defensive end, they will most likely focus on the ball. If the defensive team breaks the ball out and transitions into their offense down what was previously their defensive right side of the field, it is likely that the now-defensive team will focus the majority of their attention and players on this side of the field, which is now the defensive left side of the field and the attacking right side of the field. If the now-offensive team passes the ball behind the net and switches the play to the opposite side of the field, they will have more open space to create an offensive opportunity, which will force the defense to shift to the other side of the field.

- Players should filter into the attacking zone in waves rather than all at once. The first set of offensive players creates a fast-break option, and the second set of offensive players creates a slow-break option.

Offensive transitions can be characterized by either a fast break or a slow break. A fast break occurs when the now-offensive team is able to quickly transition into a scoring opportunity before the defense is able to fully transition back into their defensive zone, thus leaving the defense outnumbered and unsettled. A slow break occurs if the fast break does not result in an immediate offensive opportunity. After the first wave of offensive players has made the transition into the attacking zone, the second wave of offensive players still has an opportunity to use speed and space to create a scoring opportunity before the defense is fully settled. If neither the fast break nor the slow break develops into a scoring opportunity, the offensive team will move into their settled attack.

Attack Off the Fast Break

In a fast-break and person-up situation, the attacking team has the advantage and must capitalize with composure and smart decisions. On a fast break, the ball carrier can help dictate what the low attackers should do to maximize the scoring opportunity.

If the Ball Carrier Beats Her Defender   The two low attackers should maintain their positions, one on each side of the goal. This will create a 3v2 situation and force the defenders to make a decision as to who should slide. One defender will slide to the ball, and the other defender will be left with two attackers. When the defensive slide is made, the ball carrier should drift to the opposite side of where the slide came from to create more space for the low attacker who is now open. The pass should be made to the open player.

Figure 7.1 illustrates fast-break ball movement when the ball carrier beats her defender down the field. The defense is outnumbered, and a defender must shift to the ball carrier, who is the biggest threat. The ball carrier must move away from the open space, force the defense to commit to her, and then move the ball to the extra attacker who is open.

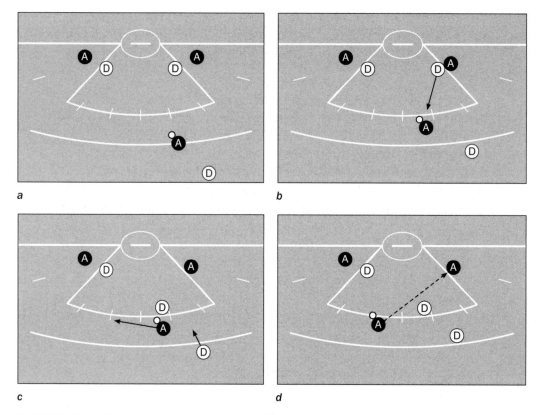

a b c d

FIGURE 7.1 Fast-break ball movement if the ball carrier beats her defender.

TIP The open attacker should run through the catch. If her feet are moving, it will be very difficult for the sliding defender to stop her.

TIP The ball carrier should pass before the defender gets to her because it will be easier to execute the pass. Waiting too long can result in a defensive interception.

If the Ball Carrier Is Even With or Slightly Ahead of Her Defender The low attacker on the ball carrier's strong side (the right side for right-handed attackers) should cut through and across the 8-meter area to give the ball carrier a chance to go 1v1 and beat the defender on her strong side (figure 7.2). The low attackers must clear the attacker's strong side because the ball carrier will have significant speed coming from the midfield. The low attackers should give her the opportunity to beat the defender 1v1.

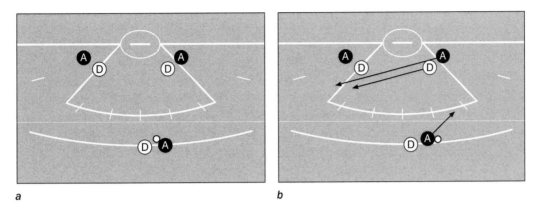

a   b

FIGURE 7.2 Fast-break movement if the ball carrier is even with or only slightly ahead of her defender. In this case, the attackers who do not posses the ball must clear one side of the field and allow the ball carrier to attack the goal 1v1.

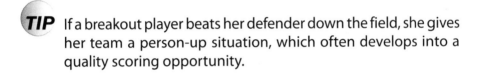 **TIP** If a breakout player beats her defender down the field, she gives her team a person-up situation, which often develops into a quality scoring opportunity.

Attack Off the Slow Break

If the breakout does not create a quality fast-break situation, attackers need to look for a slow break before settling into the attack. As described earlier, midfielders will filter into the attacking zone in waves. The first midfielders to arrive will create a potential fast break, but there will be another set of midfielders who filter in shortly thereafter and create a slow break. Keys to the slow break include the following:

- Get the ball out wide. Low attackers should cut out wide to get a pass from the ball carrier.
- Move the ball behind the net and attack. The low attacker should move the ball behind the net to the low attacker on the opposite side.
- Once behind the net, attack the opposite side and look toward the middle for open cutters coming in from the midfield.

Figure 7.3 illustrates the ball movement in a slow break. In this case, the fast break has not created a scoring opportunity, so the ball carrier moves the ball behind the net, shifts to the opposite side of the field, and looks for the second wave of offensive players who are quickly transitioning into the offensive zone.

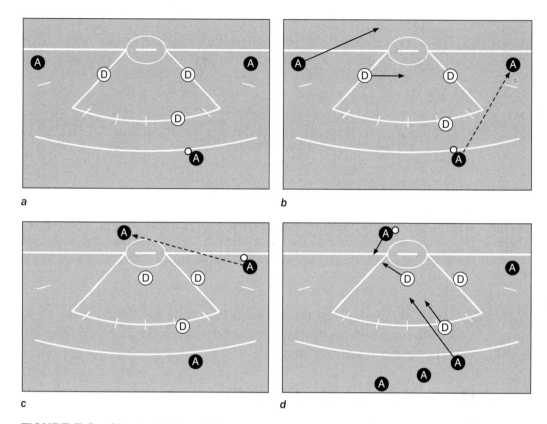

FIGURE 7.3 Slow-break breakdown.

Defensive Transitions

Similarly to what happens in an offensive transition, when a turnover occurs, the attacking team must immediately shift mentally and physically out of their offensive zone into the midfield and ultimately to their defensive zone. The now-defensive team must react to their opponent's breakout and offensive transition and do their best to prevent a fast-break situation. If a team is able to transition quickly into their defensive zone, they will hinder the transition scoring opportunities of their opponent. Defensive transition requires specific responsibilities for attackers, midfielders, and defenders. The following sections outline keys to effective defensive transitions.

Attackers' Role Attackers play a vital role in the beginning stages of transition defense. When an offensive set ends in a turnover through a goalie save, for example, it often takes attackers a second to switch gears into a defensive mindset. It is essential that attackers not let down after a turnover, missed shot, or goalie save. The attackers' job is to slow the opposing team down as they attempt to break out of their defensive zone and begin their transition offense. Attackers must play solid body defense and delay the breakout as best they can so that the rest of their team (midfielders and defenders) has time to get organized defensively. Attackers must immediately transition—mentally and physically—from offense to defense to prevent an immediate breakout and ultimately a fast-break or person-up situation for the opposing team.

Midfielders' Role The midfielders' role in transition defense is to hustle into the defensive end. Midfielders must work to beat their opponents down the field to avoid a person-up situation for the offense. This does not necessarily mean that the midfielders should turn their backs and sprint down the field. Midfielders must try to get the ball back during the breakout and redefend toward their defensive end, ready to go over the restraining line and into their settled defense. Midfielders should redefend against the opposition's midfielders, rather than against attackers, to avoid getting caught too far from the defensive end.

In certain situations, the defensive team may not be able to play a settled game of defense because they are faced with a fast or slow break and the opposing team has a person-up advantage. As described earlier in the offensive transition section, the attacking team may beat the defensive team down the field, creating an unbalanced and unsettled situation for the defense. The defense needs to remain calm, slow the ball down, prevent an immediate scoring opportunity, and allow other players to drop into the defense. The ultimate goal is to thwart a fast- or slow-break opportunity and settle into a balanced defensive situation to defend against a settled attack, rather than against a transitioning attack.

There are a variety of presses or fast-break defenses: zone, man-to-man, and so on. Following are general defensive strategies for fast-break situations that apply to different presses.

- Close the gap: Do not allow the attacker any more space than she already has. As the attacker starts to approach the 12-meter area, start to close the gap by making a move toward the attacker.

When you are a few yards from the attacker, get your feet moving in the same direction as the attacker rather than running straight at her. You will need to take a few steps forward to close the gap and then get your feet moving in the right direction. Once you have contained the attacker, get in front of her, and set up in a typical body defense position. Be ready to take away the attacker's space by getting your body in front of the attacker's body.

• Get to the stick: When you are in line with the attacker, fight to get your body in front of the attacker's stick. If you are able to get to the attacker's stick, it will slow the attacker down and force her to make a move. Make the attacker uncomfortable by preventing her from using her strong hand and taking an easy route to goal. As in a high-pressure defense, it is helpful to force the attacker to do something she does not want to do. Surprise the attacker and force her to make a bad decision.

• Play body: Do not throw stick checks in a fast-break situation. The defensive team is already down a player or two. They must play body defense and slow the attacker down to give the rest of the defense time to get back and help. Good body defense will force the attacker to make a bad decision.

During a fast break, defenders must be loud, directive, and assertive. Defenders cannot be afraid of making a wrong decision. In a fast-break situation, the only wrong decision is no decision. Following are some basic communication tips to use when defending a fast break.

• Listen to the field general: The goalie is the field general. The goalie must communicate to all of the defenders when and where to slide, and who is open. The lowest defender and the goalie must communicate the slides because they can see the entire field. They should communicate loudly and call out who should slide to ball and when the slide should occur. They must be directive and loud.

• Hustle back: Midfielders should hustle back as fast as possible and avoid drifting to the ball. Midfielders must focus on finding the open players. The low defenders need to communicate where the open person is and direct the midfielders where to go.

• Be directive: Players must be directive in their communication. The lowest defender and the goalie are the main field generals, but every player must be directive.

• Communicate: Players must communicate when they slide and where they leave. Person-down communication is the same as settled defensive communication.

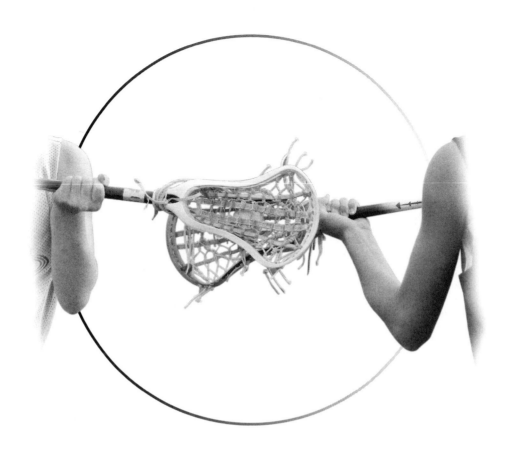

PART III

Specialty Skills

Field Players

The previous chapters discussed the basic skills, offensive skills, defensive skills, attacking concepts, and defensive concepts that, when combined, encompass the game of lacrosse. Additionally, several specialty skills are essential to a team's success. Specialty skills include draw controls, ground balls, clears and breakouts, 8-meter shots, and 8-meter defense. Many of these skills are associated with possession: The team that properly executes the skill gains possession. Possession is perhaps the most important variable in a game of lacrosse because only the team with the ball has the opportunity to score a goal. A team that is able to execute these specialty skills will have a significant advantage over the opponent.

Draw Controls

A draw control starts play at the beginning of a game and after each goal scored. The draw control, much like a face-off in hockey, occurs at the center of the field and determines possession of the ball. Two players from each team take the draw, and eight players, four from each team, stand on the circle; they will fight for the ball. Additional players behind the restraining lines also try to gain possession of the ball. The two players, one from each team, line up on their defensive side of the center line. The players hold their sticks out parallel to the ground, heads facing backward, to match up with their opponents' stick heads (figure 8.1, *a-b*). The referee places the ball in between the two players' sticks, and the players must hold this position after the referee says "ready" until the whistle is blown. When the whistle is blown, both players draw their sticks upward and away from each other (figure 8.1, *c-d*). To be legal, the trajectory of the ball must be above the heads of both players. The players who took the draw and their surrounding teammates on the circle all fight for possession of the ball (figure 8.1*e*).

Draw controls are the key to the game of lacrosse. Possession is the most defining factor in a game because a team cannot score without the ball, and winning draw controls is the best way to get control of the ball. Draw controls are the responsibility not only of the player taking the draw but also of every player who surrounds the circle and even of those behind the restraining line. The keys to successful draws are controllable: hustle, scrappiness, and determination. Players need to understand the importance of draw control and fight for the ball accordingly.

Every draw is different, and players need to be ready for the ball to go anywhere on the field. If players are spread across various sections of the field, this increases the likelihood that their team will end up with the ball. To maximize field coverage, players need to communicate positioning before, during, and after the draw control.

Players should use deception and not start out in the space where they plan to end up. If the ball tends to end up in the same space after a draw, a player can start in a different spot, anticipate the ball's movement, and run to where the ball will end up right before the whistle blows. Deception and anticipation will create an advantage and help a player beat her opposition to the ball.

FIGURE 8.1 Draw control.

Players must be persistent and remember that the draw control is not over when their team first gets the ball. Draw controls often create a number of possession changes, and a draw control is not over until one team has clear possession of the ball, away from the opposing team. A player or team must keep their guard up and battle until they have clear and safe possession of the ball. When a player controls the ball off a draw, she must stay calm and poised. The player should use protection to cradle the ball, run out of the crowded area, and find an open teammate or open space.

Players need to be flexible and adjust themselves on the circle when needed. If the draw continues to go to one side of the circle, it is helpful for players to adjust the number of players around the circle to increase the chances of getting the ball.

Ground Balls

Ground balls offer another way to gain possession. The team that picks up more ground balls than the opponent is often the team that wins the game. The keys to recovering ground balls are hustle, determination, and anticipation.

When a player goes for a ground ball, she must bend her knees to get low and scoop through the ball until it is in her stick (figure 8.2, *a-b*). Even when they get tired as the game progresses, players need to maintain this basic technique. Players should always bend their knees, scoop through the ball, cradle, and run out of a crowded ground-ball situation until they are safely away from the opposing team (figure 8.2*c*). When a player cradles, it is helpful to change the level of the cradle to make it difficult for defenders to check.

Players should always go to ground balls together. This allows one player to focus on scooping up the ground ball while the other players are ready in case the ball moves on the ground or if their teammate needs an outlet pass. Because they can never be sure which way the ball will bounce or roll, working together for a ground ball will maximize a team's opportunity to come up with the ball.

Players should always be ready for an overthrow, a missed catch, or a defensive knockdown. If a player is able to anticipate and think a few steps ahead about what might come next, she will be ready for anything and have a sure advantage over her opponent if the ball ends up on the ground.

FIGURE 8.2 Ground-ball pickup.

Clears and Breakouts

Clears and breakouts occur when the defensive team regains possession after a defensive set where a goalie makes a save, a defender creates a turnover, or the opposing team makes a mistake. As outlined in chapter 7, the movement of the ball and the defensive players out of the defensive zone is referred to as a breakout, and the shift from defense to offense is referred to as a transition. A clear is a pass or series of passes that move the ball out of the defensive zone.

The defense needs to stays poised on initial possession. It is exciting for a team to regain possession and create an opportunity to score a goal, but it is crucial to take care of the ball first. Breakouts should be calm and calculated rather than rushed or forced.

Spreading out is a key concept for players to remember during a breakout. One opposing player will be able to cover two players if they stand or run close to each other. As chapter 7 describes, the ball should be broken out, using clearing passes, down the sides of the field rather than down the middle. The ball should then be moved behind the net and to the opposite side for the offense to attack. Following are general principles that govern the roles of defenders, midfielders, and attackers during a breakout situation.

Defenders After the ball is turned over, two low defenders should immediately move to each side of the goalie for a quick, lateral, short clear. These players are essential to the start of a breakout. As a general rule, it is best to clear the ball as quickly as possible without sacrificing safe possession; this allows a team to break out before the opposing team sets up. The other two low defenders should cut out wide, near the restraining lines on each side. These defenders offer a second layer of options: further up field but still relatively close to the goalie and the defensive end. These two defenders should also be ready for a quick clear if they are open.

Midfielders Two midfielders should cut wide to each side for the next layer of the breakout. These players should be between the defensive restraining line and the 50-yard line. The third midfielder (typically the center) should go to the middle of the field. As outlined previously, although breakouts generally should not occur down the middle of the field, this midfielder is used as a connector after the ball is passed out to either side and begins to move upfield. Midfielders should start near the defensive restraining line and move downfield as the ball moves downfield.

Attackers During a breakout, two attackers should be high and two attackers should be low. The two high attackers should start near the 50-yard line in the middle of the field to allow them to run toward the ball and get open. This will also allow them to go either direction, depending on which side the ball is cleared to.

The two low attackers should be wide on each side, in between the offensive restraining line and the goal. When the ball gets to one of the low attackers, she should take the ball down her respective side; the other low attacker should run behind the net and get in a position to receive the ball. The lowest attacker should receive the ball behind the net and look to attack the opposite side. For example, if the ball is cleared down the left side of the field, the low attacker on the right side runs behind the goal, receives the ball, and looks to pass to the other attackers and midfielders who are coming into the attack down the right side of the field.

8-Meter Shots

Eight-meter shots are given to an attacking player when a major defensive foul has occurred inside the 8-meter area. After the foul is committed, the referee will set the attacker up on the 8-meter area hash mark closest to where the foul was committed. The player must stand on the hash, behind the 8-meter line, as instructed by the referee. She will receive the ball and be given the opportunity to attack the goal. All players must move 4 meters away from the ball carrier in all directions, allowing the ball carrier space and time (figure 8.3, *a-b*). After the referee has determined that all players are appropriately placed, the whistle will be blown and the attacker must explode off the line and make a decision as to how she will attack. Space, time, and defender positioning make 8-meter shots (also called free positions) great scoring opportunities. To follow are a number of techniques that will help the attacker take advantage of the opportunity.

Eight-meter shots are similar to free throws in basketball, but with significantly more defensive pressure. Much like basketball, 8-meter shots involve a mental aspect. Before a player takes an 8-meter shot, she has time to consider what to do and how best she can score a goal. It is important that a player prepare

FIGURE 8.3 8-meter shot: set-up.

the same way every time. Even if a player plans to use a different move, she should walk up to the line, stand, and focus the same way every time. If 8-meter preparation is practiced, taking the shot is no longer a variable. If a player's 8-meter preparation is second nature, she will be able to use these few seconds to consider the specific situation and how best to score a goal: what move to use, where the defense is set up, how the goalie is positioned in the net, or what the field conditions are. Consistent preparation and execution are keys to successful 8-meter shot execution.

Following are a number of guidelines for the player who is awarded an 8-meter shot.

Explode Off the Line When taking the 8-meter shot, get off the line as quickly as possible. After setting up for an 8-meter shot, look directly at the referee, who will blow the whistle. The sound of the whistle will come a split second after the referee's hand goes down. If you react to the referee's hand as the whistle blows, you will have the opportunity to get a quick start. To maximize the scoring opportunity, explode off the line with as much power as possible. Be prepared to get off the line immediately when the whistle is blown to beat the surrounding defenders to the critical scoring area. A quick start will minimize the effectiveness of the defenders and allow you to take a quality shot.

Take a Few Steps A common mistake, especially for young players, is to simply wind up and take a shot from the 8-meter without taking a step toward the goal. Scoring on a shot directly from the 8-meter takes extreme power and accuracy. Very few players, at any level, have this level of control and power on their shots from this distance. Speed is essential when running the ball in toward the goal. When the defenders start to collapse, take the shot. The 8-meter shot is now a 4-meter shot with a significantly higher chance to score.

Step Toward Space and the Goal Create as much space as possible to allow for a good shot. To create space, run forward toward the net on a diagonal. It is helpful to veer off to the opposite side of your stick. If you are right-handed, veer to the left to create space on the right side for the strong-side shot. If you are left-handed, veer to the right to create space on the left side. This movement will allow you an extra step and an extra second to get the shot off. The 8-meter area is always crowded, and defenders will be lined up to collapse and attempt to block a shot or make a stick check. An attacker who constantly changes the level of her cradle and is aware of her surrounding defenders will likely get off a quality shot.

Take Only a Few Steps Take only two or three steps before you release the shot and don't try to get too close to the goal. The longer you wait to shoot, the more likely a defender will be able to get a stick on the shot. The exact number of steps will depend on how quickly you explode off the line and your natural speed (figure 8.4a). Every shooter will have a distinct formula, and practice is the key to consistent 8-meter execution.

Be Aware of the Defense Be aware of where the defenders are positioned. Sometimes the defensive positioning prevents a shooter from executing the specific move or shot. For example, if a defender is in a position to make a quick check, you will not be able to pull your stick back to take a shot. Have a plan for executing your shot but always be ready to try something else.

Have a Plan for Each Hash   Eight-meter shots can occur at any of the seven hashes on the 8-meter. It is important to have a set plan from each hash. The best way to develop a plan is to practice repeatedly from each of the hashes. A player's strategy may differ depending on the side of the field you are on and whether you are close to the middle of the 8-meter area or toward the outside. If you are toward the middle, take the ball straight toward the goal, veering just one or two steps to the opposite of your stick (figure 8.4*b*). If you are on an outside hash, use your speed to get inside the defender and toward the middle. This will create a better angle for the shot.

Place the Shot   To have an effective 8-meter shot, calculate the placement of your shot. A player must sight the goal before she shoots, see where the goalie is in the net, and know what spots are open. Bounce shots can be very effective 8-meter shots, especially if you are farther from the goal. Regardless of where you choose to shoot, high or low, pick a spot in the net and drive the ball toward the spot (figure 8.4*c*). Shoot 6 to 8 inches (15.2-20.3 cm) inside the posts. Every shooter has a margin of error. If you aim directly for the corners, you will have a greater chance of missing the net than if you aim 6 to 8 inches inside the net.

Pass Low   Because an 8-meter shot provides an advantage to the attacking player, it is often assumed that the attacker must take the shot. This is not always the case. Attackers should also be aware of their teammates during an 8-meter shot. Defenders often are entirely focused on the ball carrier and forget about the other attackers. If another attacker is open, instead of taking the shot, pass the ball to her immediately after the whistle, giving your open teammate an opportunity for a quick shot. Especially if an attacker is open toward the bottom of the 8-meter area, look to pass immediately when the whistle is blown. A low attacker is in the best position to score a goal and should be the first option for an 8-meter shooter. The pass must come immediately, before the defense has time to cover this low attacker. If the attacker receiving the pass does not think she has a quality scoring opportunity, she should pull out and reset the attack.

Back Up the Net   Although 8-meter shots are largely individual in nature, surrounding players can help maximize the shooter's 8-meter opportunity. At least one of the shooter's teammates should plan to chase the ball if it goes behind the net. This player must anticipate, beat any defenders to the loose ball, and maintain their team's possession.

FIGURE 8.4 8-meter shot: *(a)* explode off the line, *(b)* take a few steps to create space, and *(c)* place the shot.

8-Meter Defense

Eight-meter shots present a clear advantage to the offensive team, but there are ways for the defensive team to minimize the attacker's scoring opportunity. The fundamental goal behind 8-meter defense is to do anything to disrupt the attacker's plan and deny a comfortable shot. Much like the shooter, defenders should get off the line as quickly as possible. In anticipation of the shooter's movement, the defender should run on a diagonal toward the shooter, rather than straight at her. As in any defensive situation, the defender needs to keep her stick straight up to allow for a potential knockdown. Players need to focus on solid body defense instead of swinging their sticks. The attacker will often use shot fakes to try to get the defender off balance and out of position. To disrupt the shooter's execution, the defender must explode off the line, anticipate the attacker's movement, and prevent the shooter from executing her shot cleanly.

Goalkeepers

This chapter reviews the goalkeeper's position on the field. Discussion of the goalie's position includes equipment, the ready position, steps, angles, communication, integration into practice, and the mental game. This material will be particularly useful for players who are interested in the position, and also for coaches who will benefit from an understanding of goalkeeping fundamentals and how best to incorporate this element into their overall team game plan.

Equipment

Different goalies will feel comfortable in different equipment. The ultimate purpose of goalie equipment is to protect the player from injury, and certain pieces of equipment are mandatory for safety purposes. In addition to mandatory equipment, several optional pieces are available; their use will depend on a goalie's comfort level. With increased equipment comes enhanced protection, but added equipment can also decrease flexibility and movement. The key is for the goalie to find the proper balance between protection and mobility. As a goalie becomes more experienced, she will often decrease the use of optional equipment in favor of increased mobility.

Mandatory Equipment

• Helmet: A goalie's helmet must have a built-in or attached throat protector. No part of the goalie's neck should be exposed to a potential shot.

• Gloves: It is highly encouraged that a goalie uses goalie-specific gloves, not field player gloves. The goalie position demands different protection than the field player position does. The goalie-specific glove offers extra protection for the thumb; goalies are often hit in the thumb with shots.

• Chest protector: The chest protector should cover the goalie's chest and torso area. A chest protector that is too small will leave areas exposed to a potential shot; a chest protector that is too large will be cumbersome and prone to shift, leaving exposed areas.

• Stick: The goalie's stick must be 52 to 72 inches (1.3-1.8 m) long and can have a pocket. The length of the stick should enable the goalie to easily move the stick to different locations around her body. The goalie should be very comfortable with her stick.

Optional (Recommended) Equipment

• Soccer shin guards: Soccer shin guards cover the shin area without adding significant bulk. Stepping to the ball is an essential part of goalie play, and shin guards can make a goalie less hesitant to step to the ball. If a goalie prefers not to wear shin guards during competition, she could have a pair available for practices to provide extra protection when getting many shots at once.

• Pelvic protector: This item prevents a goalie from being hit with a ball in the pelvic region.

Optional (Not Recommended) Equipment

Each of the following items is unnecessarily cumbersome, will restrict movement, and will hinder the goalie's ability to react quickly.

- Baseball or softball catcher shin pads
- Ice hockey pants
- Ice hockey shoulder pads

Ready Position

Every goalie will have a unique variation of the ready position. The ready position needs to be consistent, comfortable, and balanced; it is square one for a goalie as she prepares for a shot. As the goalie follows the play around the 8-meter area, it is important that she maintain her ready position and is prepared for a shot at all times (figure 9.1, *a-b*). Following are some basic ready position tips.

- Feet: Your feet should be shoulder-width apart, with toes pointing directly forward. Your hips are square to the ball.

- Legs: Your legs should be slightly bent in an athletic, comfortable position. Your knees should never be locked. You should be able to spring upward or sink lower when a shot comes.

FIGURE 9.1 Ready position.

- Arms: Your arms should be about a foot (.3 m) away from your body. Keep your elbows bent and away from your body to allow your arms to extend outward toward the ball.

- Hands: Your top hand should be at the very top of the stick's shaft, and your bottom hand should be about a foot lower on the shaft. The top hand should have a tight grip and will control the movement of the stick. The bottom hand should be slightly looser and more flexible, allowing the stick to move in the goalie's hands.

- Stick: Your stick should be positioned away from your head, slightly to the dominant side of the head. The stick needs to be positioned straight up, away from your head, and not tilted forward or back, to use maximum surface area.

- Weight: Your weight should be on the balls of your feet. You should be ready to explode forward, but not so much that a slight push from behind will tip you forward. Balance is fundamental to the ready position. If you are balanced in preparation for a shot, you will be in a better position to make a save.

Steps

Stepping to the ball is perhaps the most important element in goalie play. When a goalie steps to the ball, she reduces the angle of the shot and increases the chances of making a save. Stepping to the ball also forces the goalie to get her body behind the ball, which creates more surface area to make a save. If the ball gets past or deflects off her stick, the goalie's body serves as a second layer of defense. Good goalies often get hit with the ball because they step to the ball and position their bodies correctly.

Here are three basic steps to covering a shot to the left side, the right side, or straight at the goalie:

1. 45 degrees left (and forward): When a shot comes to your left side, step toward the ball on a 45-degree angle. This step should begin with the left foot, and the right foot should follow (figure 9.2a).

2. 45 degrees right (and forward): When a shot comes to your right side, step toward the ball on a 45-degree angle. This step should begin with the right foot, and the left foot should follow (figure 9.2b).

3. Straight forward: When a shot comes directly at you, step forward toward the shot. This step should begin with your dominant foot (figure 9.2c).

FIGURE 9.2 Steps: *(a)* 45 degrees left; *(b)* 45 degrees right; *(c)* straight forward.

TIP If a goalie is unsure of her dominant foot, stand behind her and push her forward with your hand. The foot she uses to catch herself as she falls forward is her dominant foot.

As the goalie steps forward, one foot should lead, and the other foot should follow immediately after the other. The step should be a comfortable distance—a significant step but not a stretch—and will be different for every goalie. The step should be quick, explosive, and assertive. The goalie's feet should remain shoulder-width apart in the ready position and never be together. The goalie should end her step in the ready position, in an athletic stance with her hips square to the ball, just as she began the step. As the goalie steps to the ball, her hands should simultaneously explode outward toward the ball. Her arms should stay bent during the step so that they can extend forward, and the goalie can drive her top hand out to the ball.

Goalies can get themselves into trouble if they do not step properly. It is important for a goalie—and her coaches—to pay attention to the goalie's stepping form and confirm that it is correct. The following guidelines can help goalies and coaches evaluate a goalie's stepping form.

• The goalie's position after the step should look much like her ready position.

• The goalie's body (shoulders and hips) should be aligned with the ball, not with the shooter's body.

• The goalie's feet should be parallel and shoulder-width apart. The trailing foot should follow immediately after the lead foot and not be left behind.

• After the step, the goalie should make the save between her shoulders (i.e., her body should be directly behind the ball).

• The goalie should begin her step immediately when the ball is released from the attacker's stick. Timing is key. If the goalie steps too soon, a savvy attacker will put the ball around the goalie and into the net. If the goalie waits too long, she will step after the shot and be much less effective. If a goalie finds she is reacting too soon, she needs to focus on being patient and waiting for the shot. If a goalie finds she does not have time to make her steps and react to the ball, she needs to focus on being more active. There is a fine line between stepping too early and too late, and it takes significant practice for a goalie to develop proper timing.

TIP For a general guideline of when to react, a goalie should focus on the moment the ball reaches the shooting strings in a shooter's stick. Most attacking players are unable to bring the ball back down into the lower pocket, and thus the shot will soon release from the stick.

Angles

The wider the shooter's angle as she approaches the net, the better chance she has to score a goal. The middle of the 8-meter area offers the biggest shooting angle and is thus the most dangerous area for a goalie. As a shooter moves toward the outside of the 8-meter area, her angle decreases, and it becomes increasingly more difficult for her to make her shot. In addition, the further a shooter is from the goal, the wider her angle will be. As she nears the net, the angle decreases. It is the responsibility of the goalie and the defense to work to minimize the angle within which the shooter can shoot. Cutting down the shooter's angle decreases her opportunity to score.

With proper positioning and steps, a goalie can decrease the shooter's angle to shoot and increase her own ability to make a save. The goalie should be lined up with the ball in the shooter's stick and should be standing in the middle of the goal as it sits behind her. If the goalie is in the middle of the shooter's angle, one step with her left foot will cover the left side of the goal, and one step with her right foot will cover the right side of the goal. As the shooter moves around the 8-meter area, the goalie must consistently adjust her position to ensure she is in the middle of the angle.

Communication

The goalie is the anchor of the defense. She is in a position to see the entire field and must direct the defense accordingly. It is the goalie's job to communicate about all aspects of play.

- Where the ball is: Although defenders should keep one eye on the ball at all times, as the goalie, you need to constantly remind the defense of the ball position by calling out phrases such as "Ball up left," "Ball behind," and "Ball middle."

- General directions: Because you have the most complete vision of the field, you are responsible for the general coordination of the defense. Often the goalie is able to see something develop before the rest of the defense and call out information: "Sarah, you have two," "Watch cutter in middle," and "Sarah, you have #7."

- Which way to force: It is up to the goalie to decide which direction the on-ball defender should force her attacker. Follow general forcing principles (see chapter 4). It is your responsibility to remind the attacker which direction to force: "Force left," "Force right."

- Slides: Because you have the best vantage point to see the defense, you are responsible for communicating who will slide to help. This communication will inform the on-ball defender that she has support, determine which supporting defender will slide, and keep the entire defense on the same page: "Sarah, you're the first slide," "Ashley, look to cover."

- Danger zone: You must quickly recognize when the attacker has reached a dangerous and threatening position. Immediately and urgently communicate the threat to the rest of the defense: "Ball's middle!" or "She's going [to goal]!"

As emphasized throughout this book, communication is the key to defense. Much of the defensive communicative and leadership responsibility falls on the goalie. It is essential that the goalie communicate effectively.

- Be directive and assertive. It is your responsibility to quarterback the defense, and you must be comfortable with this role. To control the defense, commands must be directional and persuasive.

- Use specific names and directions. The defensive zone can be hectic with many players communicating simultaneously. To increase the chances that communication will be heard and processed, refer to a specific person by name. If a name is used, there will be no confusion about who is to receive and execute the direction.

- Be decisive. You are in control of the defense, and one of the keys to defense is to make a decision and commit to it. Almost any decision can be accommodated and supported by the defensive unit as long as players commit to the decision. Half decisions or no decisions are tough to accommodate. To facilitate decisive defensive decisions, you must provide decisive direction.

- Change volume and urgency. Communication should not be monotonous. Change the volume and tone of your voice depending on the situation. You can talk in a loud, even-toned voice when communicating where the ball is. When the ball enters a danger zone, communicate very loudly, with a sense of urgency. If you change the tone and volume of your voice, you will help your teammates distinguish between different situations that call for different defensive reactions.

• Have two-way conversations. Defenders should respond to your communication and vice versa. If a defender responds to your direction, you will be confident that the direction has been received, and you will move on to the next direction, rather than repeating yourself. Two-way conversations facilitate efficient communication.

• Be consistent. You should develop a distinguishable language that other players are familiar with and respond to. Communication and directions should be consistent across practices and games to enable players to immediately understand specific communications.

Integration Into Team Practice

It can be difficult for coaches to focus individual attention on their goalies during practice, but there are various ways to involve them.

Communication is one of the most effective ways to involve a goalie in practice. The goalie should be communicating to her teammates during all playing situations. If the goalie and players communicate during practice, this will easily translate into the game. A goalie should be able to call defensive plays and be given the opportunity to make mental decisions about the defense during practice. This provides a perfect opportunity for the goalie to practice her decision making outside a pressure situation. The goalie should be at the heart of defensive communication and unity. The more integrated the goalie is, the more effective the defense will be.

It's also important for goalies to be allotted a specific time to warm up at the beginning of practice without being rushed and immediately thrown into general practice drills. The goalie should also practice specific shots during the warm-up. She should be given a repeated number of shots in specific areas. Shots should progress as follows: strong side high, weak side high, strong side middle, weak side middle, strong side low, and weak side low. The warm-up can end with repeated shots in any of the aforementioned locations. Shots should begin at approximately 75 percent speed and increase as the goalie warms up. The goalie should be warmed up by a shooter who is able to repeatedly place shots in specific locations. The goalie warm-up needs to benefit the goalie, and the warm-up shooter should focus on the goalie's specific warm-up needs.

The goalie should also integrate repetition into her warm-up time. This allows the goalie to practice similar movements and saves. The goalie position requires quick reactions; repetition creates and facilitates muscle memory, which allows the goalie to react quickly and correctly based on previous repetition.

Mental Game

Goals will be scored, and a goalie must be able to bounce back and prepare for the next opportunity to make a save. Because of the nature of the game, there is a greater chance of a goal being scored in lacrosse than in other sports. The ball is relatively small with respect to the size of the goal. Over time, progressively innovative stick design has given shooters an advantage. Shots have become increasingly dynamic and powerful. Goalies must accept that they will be scored on. Shutouts are not the reality in lacrosse that they are in hockey or soccer. The goalie should certainly strive for a shutout, but she cannot be rattled when it doesn't happen. Shutouts are a rarity in lacrosse. After a goalie is scored on, she must quickly reset mentally and avoid replaying the goal in her head. It is important to learn from mistakes, but the goalie should quickly move on and focus on the next shot.

The responsibility of the goalie is to put her team in a position to win the game, not to save every shot taken. A shutout is not necessary for winning a game. The goalie's responsibility is to direct the defense to play so that they give the goalie the best possible chance to make a save. For example, the goalie communicates to a defender to force right, and the defender is able to force the attacker to the right side of the 8-meter area. The attacker takes a low-angle shot, and the goalie makes the save. Both the defender and the goalie have done their jobs and assisted one another in doing so. The goalie needs a mindset that suppresses the notion that saves alone define successful execution.

Visualization can be a helpful tool for a goalie. If the goalie visualizes making specific saves (high shot, low shot, and so on) before a game or before practice, making those saves will become familiar. Visualization should include the three Ss: see the ball, step to the ball, and save the ball. Consistency and repetition are elements of goaltending, and visualization contributes to both.

A coach's responsibility is to get players mentally and physically prepared for any situation. A team needs a mentally sound goalie, and a coach can help build a goalie's confidence.

Certain drills are advantageous to shooters. Before such a drill, the coach can remind the goalie that the drill is not designed for goalies, and that the goalie is supposed to be scored on. Stress that saves in this particular situation are impressive.

The coach should clearly emphasize the responsibilities of the goalie to her and to the rest of the team. Make it clear to the entire team that the goalie's job is to put the team in the best position to win, not to make every save. It is the goalie's job to direct the defense and the defense's job to force low-angle, savable shots. It is the defense's job to slide early on attackers in the 8-meter area and prevent wide-open shots on goal. If the coach is clear about expectations of the goalie, the goalie will be better able to focus on her responsibilities and build confidence. A confident goalie will make the impossible save, but an unconfident goalie will have trouble making any saves at all.

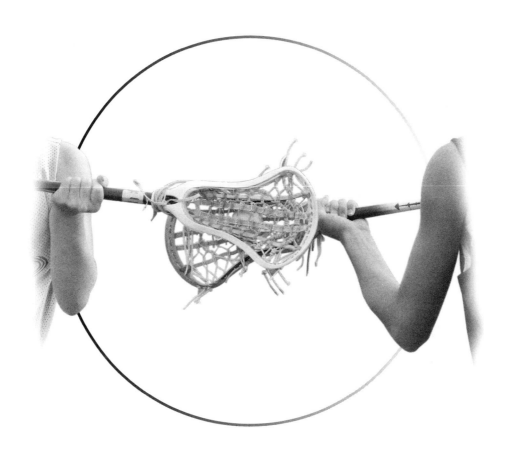

PART IV

Mastering
the Game

Situational Drills

This chapter includes several drills that provide opportunities to practice all the skills and concepts that have been detailed so far. The execution of lacrosse is progressive and cumulative; players and teams must develop a solid foundation of the basics. The drills in this chapter begin with basic skill drills and progress to more complex, small-sided concept drills, which will ultimately lead to an increased understanding and ability to put it all together and execute in a full-field game setting.

Basic Stick Skill Drills

To execute any drill, a team and its players must be able to consistently pass and catch. Once the ball is passed between players, drills will become more constructive, and the team will be able to progress toward more complex concepts and drills.

Basic stickwork is a foundation upon which all lacrosse skills, simple and complex, are built. As a player masters correct stick skills, this will become natural to them, and they will be ready to move to more advanced skills and able to handle any game situation.

At any level, it is important to continuously practice basic stick skills; if a player reverts back to old habits during a more complex situation, it is time to revisit basic stickwork! You can never practice too much, and you can always improve.

The following drills improve stickwork and passing.

PURPOSE

Partner passing is an easy way to work on a variety of stick skills. It allows players to get more comfortable having their sticks in their hands. This also serves as a good warm-up drill.

SETUP

Each player has a partner. One player lines up on the field, and her partner lines up across the field, about 7 to 10 yards (6.4-9.1 m) away. Each set of partners lines up next to each other. The entire team is in two lines, 7 to 10 yards apart.

EXECUTION

1. Players pass back and forth to each other.
2. Players work on a variety of passing and stickwork skills as directed by the coach.
   - Strong-side, weak-side, and offside catches
   - Strong-side, weak-side, and offside passes
   - One-handed and behind-the-back passes
   - Fakes: high and low, offside, around the world
   - Quicksticks
3. The coach constantly changes the skills to keep it interesting and challenging.

COACHING POINT

If players have trouble focusing or getting into partner passing, make up a routine (e.g., strong, weak, offside, one-handed, strong, behind-the-back passes) or a basic competition (e.g., how many quicksticks players can get in one minute).

PURPOSE

Nothing in lacrosse is stationary. Partner passing on the move will help players coordinate footwork with stick skills. This drill also serves as a good warm-up for players.

SETUP

Line players up in groups of two about 5 to 7 yards (4.6-6.4 m) apart.

EXECUTION

1. The coach picks a stickwork skill and a footwork skill (e.g., weak hand passing with a shuffle step).
2. Players run down the length of the field passing back and forth to each other while executing the stickwork and footwork skills.
3. When one pair of players has run about 10 yards (9.1 m), the next group of players begins.

COACHING POINT

Initially, the primary focus is on correct execution, not speed. Players should be able to execute both the stickwork and footwork skill before they increase their speed.

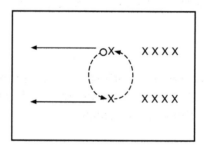

PURPOSE

Three-man partner passing on the move allows for more advanced stick work on the move and allows players to work on protection on the move. This drill serves as a great warm-up.

SETUP

Players split into groups of three and line up on the end line in a triangle, all facing forward. The top of the triangle points toward the front.

EXECUTION

1. All three players begin to run forward.
2. The player in front receives a pass over her shoulder (catching offside), turns her torso toward her strong side (keeping feet facing forward), and passes to the other partner.
3. This partner then passes back to the player in front, who now catches the ball over the strong-side shoulder. She then turns her torso toward her offside and passes offside to the player who started with the ball.
4. The entire drill is done on the move. Every pass and catch occurs with the players' feet moving forward.

COACHING POINT

Before they make a pass offside or strong side, it is important that your players adjust their wrists and hands so their knuckles are facing outward. Players do not turn around to make the pass. Movement will continue forward, and only the players' hands and wrists will adjust to make the backward pass.

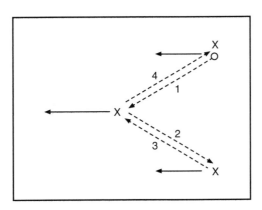

PURPOSE

This is a good drill to work on fast ball movement, a key to a good attack and successful midfield.

SETUP

Players break into groups of four and line up in a square.

EXECUTION

1. Players pass the ball as quickly as possible around the square, limiting cradles.
2. Players catch and throw with their outside hands. For example, if a player receives the ball from the right side, she should make the catch with her right hand. She then must pivot and switch the ball to her left hand to make the pass. This will ensure that the pass is made with the outside hand. Players must use both right and left hands.

COACHING POINT

The purpose of using the outside hand and of switching hands is to work on added protection. If players turn to the outside, rather than into the middle of the circle, they will use their bodies to protect their stick as they make passes.

PURPOSE

This drill helps the attack work on popping out to support the ball. This skill is a key fundamental to any attacking offense.

SETUP

Players split into groups of three and line up in a triangle setting. One player has the ball; the other two are supporting players on either side.

EXECUTION

1. Players pass the ball around as quickly as possible.
2. The attacker who does not receive the ball must cut through to the other side to support the player who receives the ball.
3. No matter where the ball is passed, there must always be an attacker on each side supporting the ball. The ball carrier should always be at the point of the triangle, with support on both sides.
4. When players become comfortable with the movement, add defenders to the drill.

COACHING POINT

Start by using only two defenders (one on ball and one off ball). This will emphasize how important it is to support both sides of the ball because only one player will be open each time. If the player who does not receive the ball cuts to the opposite side of the ball carrier, there will always be an open pass. When players get really good at the drill, add a third defender. This will force all offensive movement to be done with pressure.

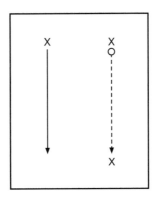

Protection Drills

It is very important for a player to be able to protect her stick. If players are able to protect their sticks from the defenders around them, they will maximize possession and minimize turnovers.

As discussed throughout the book, possession is essential to success in lacrosse. Stick skills are the root of possession. A team with players who can effectively pass, catch, and protect their sticks will be better able to maintain possession.

Protection requires an awareness of your own stick and of everything going on around you. During any game situation, the player with the ball is the primary focus of an opposing team and its defenders. If this player can protect her stick under pressure and safely move the ball while maintaining composure, she will contribute to a controlled and effective unit.

Protection is important across all positions—attack, midfield, defense, and goalie—and across all game situations. The following drills focus on protection, both stationary and on the move.

PURPOSE

Stationary protection develops the basics of stick protection in a limited-movement situation. Players must learn to keep their heads on a swivel and protect their sticks with a limited amount of movement before they are able to do so when on the move.

SETUP

Players split into groups of two and work directly in front of or behind their partners. One player is the attacker with the ball, and the other player is the defender.

EXECUTION

1. The attacker possesses the ball and works on protecting her stick to prevent the defender from checking the stick. The attacker is only allowed to pivot with one foot; she cannot run away from the defender.
2. The defender stands behind or in front of the attacker and tries to check the attacker's stick. The defender can only move in the limited space as well; she cannot run around the attacker and can only move roughly one foot (.3 m) in any direction.
3. The attacker and defender switch positions and repeat the drill.

COACHING POINT

The attacker should always keep her body between the defender and her own stick with the ball. The attacker must keep her head up and on a swivel. If the attacker can see the defender and her stick, she will need to make only a limited amount of cradles to protect the stick—there is no need to go crazy.

PURPOSE

Players work on protecting their stick in a game speed situation. This drill works on coordinating footwork with stickwork.

SETUP

Players split into groups of two and work directly in front of or behind their partners. One player is the attacker with the ball, and the other player is the defender.

EXECUTION

1. The defender starts in front of the attacker and allows the attacker to beat her.

2. Using walking speed to start, the attacker walks 20 yards (18.3 m) down the field, protecting her stick while the defender tries to get off a back check.

3. After a couple of repetitions, the attacker increases her speed to a run. The defender runs behind the attacker and tries to check the attacker's stick.

4. The attacker and defender switch positions and repeat the drill.

COACHING POINT

Add a third player to the drill (see diagram). The third player will act as the passer and will make a pass to the attacker to start the drill. This pass will force the attacker to catch the ball in front of her and between her shoulders to protect her stick. The attacker then runs around the defender, protecting her stick, and ends the repetition with a pass back to the third player, which forces the attacker to keep her head up and make a clean pass between her shoulders.

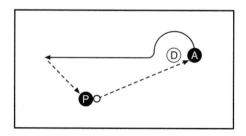

PURPOSE

Three-man partner passing on the move allows players to use more advanced stickwork on the move and work on protection on the move. This drill serves as a great warm-up.

SETUP

Players set up in groups of three and line up on the end line. One player starts 5 to 7 yards (4.6-6.4 m) in front, facing the other partners. This player is the passer. The other two line up one in front of the other.

EXECUTION

1. The passer passes with the second player who is lined up directly in front of the third player.
2. The second player must pass to and receive passes from the passer while protecting her stick from the player behind her.
3. The player behind is the defender; she looks for back checks and forces the player in front to protect her stick. She will remain behind the second player for the duration of the drill.
4. This drill can be done as a stationary drill to start. After players become comfortable, all three players should be moving while executing the drill. The passer will backpedal, while the second and third players run forward.

COACHING POINT

The attacker, who is the second player, must keep her head on a swivel, looking back at the defender to see where her stick is. The attacker must make her stick change levels. She must focus on catching and passing the ball inside her shoulders and in front of her body for increased protection.

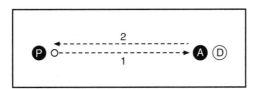

PURPOSE

This drill creates a game situation in which the attacker gets doubled while taking a 1v1. The attacker must pull out of pressure, keep her head up, and make a good pass. The other attackers must pop out to support the ball; this is a basic and key attacking concept.

SETUP

Players split into three defenders and three attackers. The three attackers form a triangle and stand 7 to 10 yards (6.4-9.1 m) away from each other. Each defender picks up an attacker.

EXECUTION

1. The ball starts with one player at the point of the triangle, and a supporting attacker on each side.
2. The attacker with the ball chooses a side and goes 1v1 (at speed).
3. The supporting defender on that side slides early to the double-team.
4. When the attacker feels the pressure from the double-team, she pulls out of the double by turning around and running out of the double-team.
5. Simultaneously, the open attacker pops out to support the ball.
6. The ball carrier then makes a pass to the open attacker who has popped out to support the ball.
7. The open attacker receives the ball and makes a second pass to end the drill.

COACHING POINT

Have the defenders slide early and hard on the double. Once in a while, have the other supporting defender change which attacker she leaves open. This will force the attacker in the double-team to keep her head up and find the open pass under pressure.

If the attackers master this, add a fourth defender (see diagram). Now everyone will be marked and there will be an automatic double. This will help emphasize the importance of popping out to support the ball.

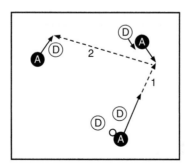

Shooting Drills

The goal of lacrosse is to score, and players need to understand that scoring opportunities are limited. Efficient shooting comes with practice and repetition.

Players should practice shooting from all different angles and using all different shots—low, high, and bounce. Different shots will be more effective in different game situations; players may prefer one type of shot over another, but it is important to practice and be comfortable with all of them. For example, a player may face a goalie who is very good against bounce shots, and she must be able to adjust and shoot elsewhere. It is also important to be comfortable shooting with both hands. A player who can take all different types of shots with both hands will be a significant scoring threat and offensive asset.

Players should focus on proper shooting form, as described previously, and on accuracy over power. As a player becomes consistently accurate with her shots, she can begin to increase power. Often, though, accuracy coupled with deception will be enough to score a goal.

The following drills are for shooting practice.

PURPOSE

This simple drill provides players with multiple shooting repetitions from various areas and with both hands. It also allows players to shoot at game speed and with defense.

SETUP

Players break into two lines, one on each corner of the 8-meter area. Designate one line as passers and the other line as shooters.

EXECUTION

1. The first player in the passing line begins about halfway down the outside line of the 8-meter area and runs with the ball toward the corner of the 8-meter area and the shooting line.
2. Simultaneously, the first player in the shooting line makes a hard cut toward to player with the ball.
3. The player in the passing line feeds the ball to the attacker who is cutting toward her.
4. The shooter catches the ball with her outside hand (relative to the goal) and takes a shot on goal.
5. The drill is repeated with the next passer and shooter. Players go as fast as possible, allowing the goalie to be set for each shot.
6. The balls switch to the other line, and the shooting line becomes the passing line. This forces players to shoot right-handed and left-handed.
7. The lines then move: One line moves behind the net, and the other moves to the top of the 8-meter area to work on high and low shooting.

COACHING POINT

When players get comfortable shooting, add a trailing defender on the shooter. This will force players to cut at full speed and not slow down to catch or shoot. A defender can also be added on the passer.

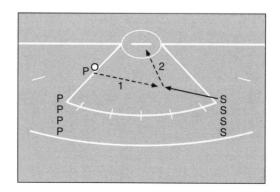

PURPOSE

The drill allows shooters to get repetitions from both high and low. It also allows players to work on quick ball movement around the circle.

SETUP

Players split into four lines: two lines on each side of the top of the 8-meter area and two lines low on each side of the goal.

EXECUTION

1. The ball starts on the top right corner.
2. Players pass the ball around the square in a counterclockwise rotation: top right, to bottom right, to bottom left, to top left.
3. The last player (top left) cuts in toward the middle of the 8-meter area to receive the pass from the bottom left player and take a shot.
4. Players repeat the drill with the ball starting in each corner.
   - Ball starts high left; pass clockwise; high right shoots
   - Ball starts low right; pass clockwise; low left shoots
   - Ball starts low left; pass counter clockwise; low right shoots

COACHING POINT

Make sure players pop out to the ball, catch, and pass with the outside hand and make crisp, quick passes. This drill should be done quickly, one repetition after another, but not to the point that it gets sloppy.

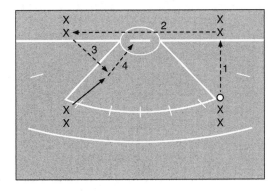

PURPOSE

This drill combines high and low shots into one drill.

SETUP

Players split into three lines: one line at the top of the 8-meter, one line low to the left side of the goal, and one line on the right wing of the 8-meter area.

EXECUTION

1. Balls start low and on the right wing.
2. The low player passes to the top player who is cutting to goal.
3. The top player receives the ball and takes a shot.
4. The low player who has just passed the ball waits until the shot is taken and then cuts around the front of the crease and receives a pass from the wing. The low player shoots, and that repetition ends.
5. The drill starts again when the low player passes to the top player who is cutting to goal.
6. After a few rounds, the low and wing lines move to the opposite sides.

COACHING POINT

Remind players to use their outside hands to pass and cut. The low attacker should make her cut well away from the crease, allowing herself room to make a fake and then take a shot without crossing into the crease.

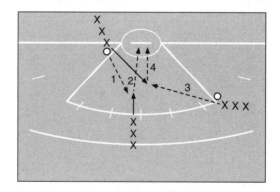

PURPOSE

This drill helps players work on setting and using the pick. Players also work on making quick catches and shots off the pick (both right- and left-handed).

SETUP

Players split into four lines, two high and two low (just as in the Four Corners shooting drill).

EXECUTION

1. The balls start at the top right and move counterclockwise.
2. The player at the top right makes a pass to the player on the bottom right.
3. After the top right player makes the pass, she runs to the top of the 8-meter area and sets a pick for the top left player.
4. Simultaneously, the ball moves behind the net from the bottom right player to the bottom left player.
5. As the ball moves behind the net, the top left player times her cut so she comes off the pick just as the low left player receives the ball and gets ready to feed.
6. The top left player runs off the pick and looks to receive the ball and shoot.
7. After the top right player sets the pick, she rolls off and cuts behind the first cutter to offer a second option. If the first cutter does not receive the ball, the second cutter receives the ball and shoots.
8. The drill begins again with a pass from the top right to the bottom right.

COACHING POINT

In a pick situation, it is the responsibility of the person coming off the pick to use it effectively. Timing is everything. The cutter must be patient and cut hard.

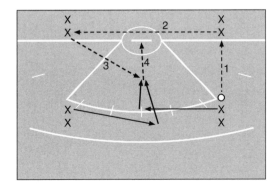

Concept Drills

When players become competent with basic passing, protection, and shooting drills, they are ready to move to the next level. Concept drills use small-sided game setups to simulate various situational aspects of a full game. Concept drills are a step in the progression toward full-field game play and are helpful in breaking bigger concepts into smaller pieces.

If players are just beginning lacrosse, concept drills introduce more complex elements of the game and will help increase their comfort levels before they are faced with a full-field game situation. For more experience players, concept drills break the game down and provide the opportunity to focus on and improve specific scenarios.

Certain essential game concepts—space, timing, and movement—are best practiced in a small-scale setting. When players become proficient and comfortable, they are ready to keep building upon the concepts and ultimately will be prepared for the full-field game situation. It is very important to simulate a game situation during concept drills.

PURPOSE

This drill helps players practice 1v1s offensively and defensively in a gamelike situation, right off the pass.

SETUP

Players break into four lines of attack and four lines of defense. One line is behind the goal, one is at the top of the 8-meter area, and one is on each wing. There are balls in each line.

EXECUTION

1. The line at the top of the 8-meter area starts the drill.
2. The line on the right wing passes the ball to the attacker who is cutting toward the ball at speed.
3. The attacker uses the speed from her cut to go 1v1 against the defender in front of her.
4. The next attacker in the top line passes the ball to the attacker cutting from the line on the left wing.
5. The attacker cuts toward the ball and goes 1v1 against the defender in front of her.
6. The drill rotates clockwise around the lines so that each attacker receives the ball from the line to her right.
7. Players repeat the drill in a counterclockwise direction, which forces attackers to catch the ball with their left hands.

COACHING POINT

Make sure to work the 1v1 with defense pressuring out and then with defense sagging in. Make sure the players are aggressive both offensively and defensively.

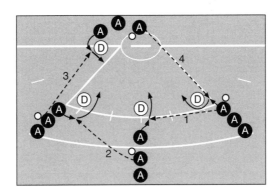

PURPOSE

This drill allows players to work on the fundamentals of working together to set picks and get open. Picks can be a difficult concept for players to grasp, and this drill helps players practice in a small-sided setting.

SETUP

Two attackers and two defenders set up on one side of the 8-meter area, with a passer set up on the opposite side. This allows the attackers the space to set picks and make cuts toward the ball. The passer should set up between the goal line and the corner of the 8-meter area.

EXECUTION

1. The two attackers work together to set picks for each other until one is able to get open and cut toward the passer.
2. If an attacker gets open, the passer can hit her with the pass, and the attacker can go to goal.

COACHING POINT

This is also a good drill for the defense. Make sure the defensive players communicate through the picks. The attackers need to be patient and communicate as well. A pick is not a secret play; it is okay to communicate about it with teammates. Note that it may take more than one pick to open up the attacker enough for her to make an open cut to receive the ball.

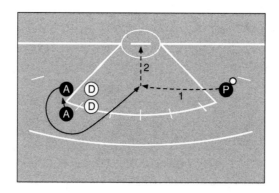

PURPOSE

This drill gives players the space to work on a fast-break situation from the restraining line.

SETUP

Three attackers start along the restraining line and two defenders start low, inside the 8-meter area. There is a line of players behind each position.

EXECUTION

1. The goalie picks an attacker to clear to and starts the drill.
2. The three attackers transition into the offensive zone and go to goal.
3. The attackers have a man-up advantage and should stay spread, attack the middle of the field, and force the defense to decide who to mark.
4. The drill ends when one of the attackers takes a shot (goal or no goal) or when one of the defenders causes a turnover.
5. The next three attackers step up to the restraining line, the next two defenders step into the 8-meter area, and the drill begins again.

COACHING POINT

Attackers should go hard to goal to keep the defense honest and force them to commit to the attacker with the ball. If the attacker can beat the defender, she should go hard to goal.

3v2 drills simulate a man-up situation. The same concepts should be used to create space and force one defender to pick up the ball, leaving the other defender with two attackers.

There are innumerable combinations. The key is to go hard to goal, open space with cuts, and move the ball to the open player.

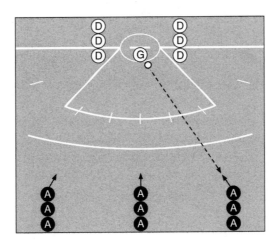

PURPOSE

In this drill, players work on a man-up situation inside the 8-meter area. This changes the focus from speed to skill because players need to make crisp passes, throw in fakes, and be aggressive. In a small space, deception is the most effective weapon.

SETUP

Two attacking lines and two defensive lines start low, with one line on each side of the net. A third line of attackers starts at the top of the 8-meter area.

EXECUTION

1. The drill starts when the top attacker takes a warm-up shot on the goalie from just inside the 8-meter area.
2. The goalie clears the ball to this same attacker, who then cuts away from the goal toward the top of the 8-meter area.
3. The top attacker catches the ball and the 3v2 to goal starts.
4. All three attackers work within the 8-meter area to score a goal.

COACHING POINT

This drill does not allow for a lot of movement or space. The attackers must use deception to open up teammates and shots.

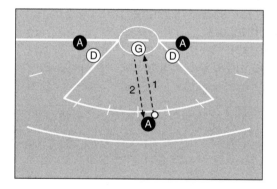

PURPOSE

This drill works on both sides of the transition: breaking the ball out of the defensive zone and attacking on the fast break.

SETUP

Three attacking lines start across the restraining line. There is one defender on each side of the goal and a shooter at the top of the 8-meter area (this can be a coach).

EXECUTION

1. The shooter at the top of the 8-meter area pops out to receive a clear from the goalie and then takes an outside shot.
2. The two defenders break wide on either side of the net for the goalie clear.
3. The defender who receives the ball looks to pass the ball to one of the attackers who is cutting in from the restraining line wings.
4. The attacker who receives the ball moves it to the middle line attacker, and the 3v2 starts.
5. The three attackers go to goal against the two defenders. The shooter is now out of the play.

COACHING POINT

Make sure players move the ball crisply and make hard cuts toward the ball. There is no defense on the breakout, but it should not be done lazily.

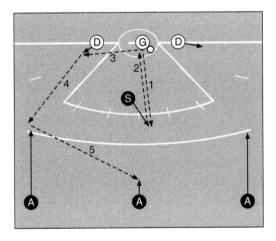

PURPOSE

This drill works on defensive sliding and communication. It also works on attackers' ball movement and deception.

SETUP

Start with four attackers in a box inside the 8-meter area, two high and two low. Three defenders should be lined up: one on the ball, one on the adjacent attacker on the same side as the ball, and one guarding the two attackers on the opposite side.

EXECUTION

As the attackers move the ball around the box looking for a good shot, the defenders communicate and slide to stop them.

COACHING POINT

There are innumerable combinations for ball movement. Attackers should make cuts and set picks to create space. The ball should move around the box, forcing defenders to slide to the open player.

Tell your defenders to make quick decisions and slide. As long as they communicate, they will be okay. Have players be as directive as possible in their communication (e.g., "Sarah, slide low" or "I am leaving, so watch low right").

The drill works on defensive sliding and communication and also acts as a conditioning drill. Because there are only three defenders and four attackers, the defenders will be constantly moving and shifting. Defensive communication and decision making become increasingly challenging as defenders get tired, and this drill helps simulate a real game situation.

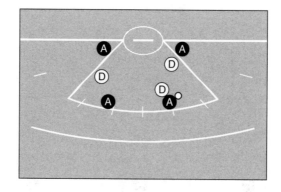

PURPOSE

This drill will help give attackers a basic motion that serves as the basis for most plays. It will help attackers understand the concept of cutting through to open up space for the 1v1 and popping out to support the ball.

SETUP

Four attackers and four defenders spread out around the attacking zone: one high, one low, and one on either wing. The ball starts high with a 1v1.

EXECUTION

1. The attacker on the right wing cuts through the 8-meter area to the left side to open up space for the 1v1.
2. The defender on the right wing has the option of sliding to the attacker up top who plans to go 1v1 or following her attacker through to the left side of the 8-meter area.
3. The attacker up top looks to go 1v1 toward the right side, where the space has been cleared.
4. If the attacker does not have the 1v1, she pulls out and makes a pass to one of the other two attackers who are popping out to support the ball on both sides.
5. The ball carrier should move the ball to the opposite side (by passing or running it if she is behind the net) and then attack the opposite side.

COACHING POINT

If the ball carrier is doubled, she should not feed the ball into the middle. It may seem open momentarily, but this is not a good option. The attacker should move the ball to one of her side outlets who can then either attack or hit the open player in the middle.

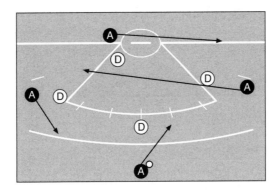

PURPOSE

The objective of this drill is to have the defense force the attacker to her defensive help. The defender must do everything in her power to force the attacker to help, and the defender's slide must come early.

SETUP

Two attackers and two defenders start behind the goal on either side. One attacker and one defender set up on the left wing, and one attacker and defender set up at the top.

EXECUTION

1. The attacker up top has the ball and tries to take the 1v1 right-handed.
2. The defender must step up to that side and force the attacker back to the right where the defender's help is.
3. Simultaneously, the defender on the wing is ready to slide early to help with the 1v1.
4. The low defender on that same side is ready to slide up to help with the attacker left behind by the first sliding defender.

COACHING POINT

Communication and anticipation are the keys. The 1v1 defender needs to do everything to force the attacker to the right, back toward the defensive help. This defender may get beaten, and the slide from the defender on the right needs to come very early.

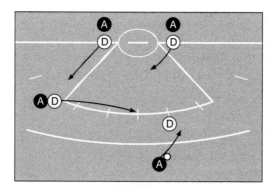

Goalie Drills

The following drills are specific to the goalie and are beneficial to both goalies and their coaches. Some of the drills can be done by the goalie alone, but others need a coach or partner. Goalies should practice drills that break down the elements of that position rather than simply participate in shooting drills with teammates.

Positioning, steps, angles, eye–hand coordination, and timing are essential to goalie success. It is important to break down the goalie position into situations that allow for practice of each of the aforementioned elements. During goalie drills, the goalie should start by focusing on a specific element—steps, for example—rather than all elements at once. When a goalie becomes comfortable with her steps, she can build on this and focus on timing, and so on.

Repetition is essential to create muscle memory. If a goalie's steps and angles become second nature, she will be able to focus on reacting to make saves rather than on her technique.

PURPOSE

This drill works on the simple movement of the goalie around the crease. Developing a comfortable and consistent movement pattern around the crease will allow the goalie to focus on making the save, not just on using the proper footwork.

SETUP

The goalie starts at one post as if she is prepared for a shot from the goal line extended.

EXECUTION

1. The goalie begins taking steps in a semicircle all the way around the crease so that she ends up at the opposite post.
2. The number of steps depends on the goalie, but the key is consistency. The goalie should take exactly the same route around the crease each time; she should end up at the opposite post each time, facing the opposite goal line extended.

COACHING POINT

The more the goalie practices, the more comfortable the movement will become. Eventually, have her do it with her eyes closed.

PURPOSE

This drill helps the muscle memory needed to step to the ball on every shot. Making this move will become natural, and during a game, the goalie won't need to think about which foot to step with.

SETUP

The goalie starts in the ready position without her stick. Her strong hand is out in front, and her other hand is behind her back.

EXECUTION

1. A partner or coach tosses the ball to the goalie.
2. The goalie steps out to the ball at a 45-degree angle and catches it.
3. The goalie should catch the ball in front of her body, between her shoulders, and at the farthest point she can reach, rather than wait until the ball gets close to her body.

COACHING POINT

Have your goalie start behind a line so you can be sure she is stepping forward and not waiting for the ball to come to her.

PURPOSE

This drill has the goalie practice a physical routine and a simultaneous mental task. The physical routines should become natural, and the goalie should also be able to complete mental tasks.

SETUP

A different-colored strip is taped around each of four balls. The goalie starts with her back to her partner, in her ready position.

EXECUTION

1. The partner says, "Go," and the goalie turns around, steps toward the ball, and calls out the color of the tape as she catches it.
2. Repeat the drill a number of times; the partner continues to throw the balls, and the goalie continues to take the same steps from backward to forward in the ready position.

COACHING POINT

The goalie should be stepping forward, catching the ball, and saying the color simultaneously. Have the goalie start behind a line to make sure she is stepping forward.

PURPOSE

The purpose of this drill is to ensure that the goalie is stepping to the ball, getting her hands out, and making the save between her shoulders. The drill develops eye–hand coordination.

SETUP

The goalie stands in her ready position, with her equipment on but without her stick. She should hold either a shaft or a field player's stick turned upside down. She should hold the shaft toward the bottom and straight up, just as she would hold her goalie stick.

EXECUTION

1. The partner or coach stands about 4 yards (3.7 m) away from the goalie and uses a lacrosse stick to throw tennis balls at the goalie.

2. The goalie plays as she usually would but must use the shaft to save the tennis balls.

3. The goalie must step to each ball and save it between her shoulders. It is much more difficult to make solid contact with a skinny shaft than with a full stick head. The goalie will need to use her body to back up the shots she misses with the shaft.

4. As the goalie begins to develop her eye–hand coordination and get comfortable, the partner or coach can move around to other locations and shoot harder.

COACHING POINT

If the goalie cannot get her hands to the ball quickly enough, her body should still be there to block it. If this is not the case, then she is just poking at the ball with her stick. Rebounds should bounce back to where the shooter shot from. This shows the goalie is stepping to the ball. If rebounds are to the side, then the goalie is stepping flat or sideways.

PURPOSE

This drill will help the goalie work on her turns and her ability to find the ball quickly to make a save.

SETUP

Have the goalie start in the crease with her back to the shooter. The shooter should stand about 7 yards (6.4 m) in front of the crease.

EXECUTION

1. The coach says, "Go," and the goalie turns around and gets into her ready position.
2. The shooter takes a quick shot. The shooter should give the goalie time to get into her ready position but make sure the goalie is being quick and stepping forward.
3. The goalie steps to the ball, makes the save, passes it back to the coach.
4. The goalie turns around and repeats the drill.

COACHING POINT

The shooter should continue to move around and shoot at various places so that the goalie needs to find the shot when she turns around.

PURPOSE

This drill allows the goalie to work on multiple fundamentals all at once: clearing, handling ground balls, moving in and out of the crease, and making the save.

SETUP

The goalie starts in the crease. A coach should stand about 7 yards (6.4 m) in front of the crease. Another coach or player should stand about 25 yards (22.9 m) away from the goalie, in any direction.

EXECUTION

1. One coach or player rolls a ball to one side of the crease.
2. The goalie runs out of the crease, picks up the ground ball, and clears to the other player or coach.
3. After the clear, the goalie quickly gets back in the goal for a quick shot from the other coach or player.

COACHING POINT

The drill should not be rushed. The goalie should be making accurate clears and have enough time to get back into her ready position before the next shot. At the same time, she should be moving quickly. The person receiving the clears should move around so the goalie is forced to find her and have to clear to different places each time. Even if the goalie is tired, make sure she continues to step forward to make the saves.

Stick Tricks

Stick tricks are fun and can also be effective in increasing a player's stickwork and comfort level with her stick. Any challenging maneuver with the stick can be considered a stick trick. As with any skill or concept, the more a player practices, the better she will become. When a player is able to master a challenging stick trick, she will not only have a cool trick to show her teammates, but she will have become increasingly comfortable with her stick. As that comfort level increases, she will find her stick skills and overall game will improve. This chapter describes the steps for nine stick tricks.

THE TRICK

A player spins the stick and ball like a baton above her head from one side of her body to the other and catches one-handed; all the while the ball remains in the stick.

EXECUTION

1. Begin by holding the stick and ball one-handed at the right side of your body about hip level and parallel to the ground. Your right hand should be anywhere between the middle and the base of the shaft, and your left hand should be at your left side.

2. In one motion, bring your right arm up and, as if revving a motorcycle throttle, flick your wrist toward your left side and release the shaft up and over your head. Be sure that your motorcycle flick is even enough to keep the stick parallel to the ground even when it is flying over head.

3. Keep your eyes on the stick as it twirls over head. As soon as you spot the stick in midair with its head facing the ground, take your left hand and grab the shaft toward the outside, completing the rainbow shape.

COACHING POINTS

· Make sure the player's shaft remains parallel to the ground throughout the entire trick (even when above her head!). This will prevent the ball from flying out.

· If the motorcycle flick is too erratic, show the player how to use her left hand to stabilize the stick by placing it beneath the shaft, palm down and just below the head of the stick (see sequence on page 154). The left hand follows the stick through the previously mentioned steps and turns it outward and toward the left to go straight into the left-hand grab.

Rainbow stick trick.

(continued)

Rainbow stick trick with stabilizing hand.

VARIATIONS

With a Partner

Stand shoulder to shoulder with a partner. By using more power in the rainbow flip, one partner can do the overhead flipping with her outside hand while the other one catches with her outside hand (see sequence on page 155).

Back and Forth

Once you've perfected the rainbow from right to left, you can do the same trick from left to right and flip back and forth continuously.

Rainbow stick trick with partner.

THE TRICK

A player spins in a circle with both the stick and the ball perpendicular to the ground, using centrifugal force to keep the ball in the stick.

EXECUTION

1. Start by holding the stick at the base of the shaft just as you would if you were cradling one-handed. Hold the stick almost perpendicular to the ground but with the base of the shaft angled slightly away from your body. Keep the head facing in toward your body so that the ball doesn't roll out.

2. While maintaining the slight angle on the stick, begin to spin in a tight circle to your left side.

3. As you begin to increase the speed of your tight-circle spin, you can begin to straighten out the angle so that the stick is now completely perpendicular to the ground, making the ball seem as if it were glued to your strings.

COACHING POINT

If a player is having trouble starting the spin without the ball flying out, have the player turn the head of her stick slightly toward the direction in which she is spinning.

VARIATION

Once you've perfected spinning in a full circle, you can do the same trick while standing still and spinning back and forth 180 degrees (instead of a full 360 degrees), changing direction from left to right, and from in front of your body to behind your back.

THE TRICK

A player makes a bounce pass from behind her back and in between her legs to a partner.

EXECUTION

1. Begin by holding the stick with a ball in it, using both hands. Your hands should be close together and toward the base of your shaft. Hold the stick parallel to the ground and behind your head as if you are going to make a huge over-the-head pass. The base of the shaft, and your hands, should be directly over your head; the head of the stick should be straight out, parallel to the ground and behind your body.

2. In one swift motion, rotate the shaft and head of your stick to the right so the head of your stick rotates to face the ground. As you turn the stick to make a downward pass, bring the stick toward your body and follow through with the head of the stick facing forward, in between your legs, from behind your back.

COACHING POINT

If a player is having trouble and too often smacks herself in the back, have her try standing on the tips of her toes just before she makes the downward motion.

THE TRICK

A player picks up the ball one-handed in a magically swift motion without scooping from beneath or raking back the ball.

EXECUTION

1. Begin by holding your stick one-handed toward the bottom of the shaft. Put a ball on the ground in front of you.

2. By using the top left corner of the stick's head, rotate your wrist to the left, come over top of the ball, and get slightly underneath it. Use your wrist to flick the ball slightly upward, off the ground.

3. Once the ball is in the air (about 1 to 2 inches [2.5 to 5.1 cm] off the ground), turn your wrist back to the right, come underneath the hovering ball, and grab to catch it.

COACHING POINTS

· If a player has trouble controlling the stick from the bottom of the shaft, have her choke up and start with one hand about halfway up the shaft, closer to the head of the stick. As the player masters the trick, gets stronger, and gains more control of her stick, she can move her hand back down toward the bottom.

· Cushy grass is often an easier surface on which to learn the trick than turf or pavement because the grass elevates the ball slightly.

VARIATION

The same trick can also be done from front to back. Follow the same steps but keep your stick vertical, or perpendicular to the ground. Flick the ball toward your feet with the stick head facing you. Then rotate your wrists so that the stick head faces away from you and allow the ball to either flick or roll into the head.

THE TRICK

A player pops the ball to herself and catches the ball by balancing it on the sidewall of the head of the stick.

EXECUTION

1. Begin with the stick in your strong hand with a ball in the pocket as if you are cradling low in front of your body.
2. Very lightly toss the ball up in the air. The toss should be a light wrist flick, or a pop. Make sure you do not pop the ball too high; the higher the pop, the more difficult it is to catch.
3. Turn the head of your stick so that the sidewall is facing up toward the sky, toward the ball that has been popped into the air. Raise the stick upward in that position and meet the ball you have just popped up in the air. When the ball and the sidewall of the stick are about to meet, give with the stick as though you are catching an egg or water balloon.

COACHING POINTS

- When a player is popping the ball up in the air, make sure she releases the ball straight upward from the pocket of her stick; if the ball rolls out of the top of the stick when it is popped, the ball will begin to spin, making it more difficult to catch.

- Some sticks perform this trick better than others because of their sidewall design. To test out the best place to catch the ball on the sidewall, the player should use her hand to place the ball on the side of the stick and try to balance the ball. If the ball stays on the side of the stick and is balanced, the player will be able to catch it in that spot with enough practice.

VARIATIONS

The Magnet

This variation creates an effect where the ball seems to be glued to the sidewall.

1. Once you've caught or placed the ball on your sidewall, hold the stick in one hand at the base of the shaft and place it to one side of your body. (If you are right-handed, it sometimes is easier to start on the left side so that you end up with your right arm across your body.)

2. Raise your arm and bring the stick from one side of your body to the other, making sure that the head of the stick is underneath the ball at all times. When you bring your stick from one side to another, your elbow should remain fairly stationary.

(continued)

The Roll

In this variation, after you have caught the ball on the sidewall, roll the ball down the shaft and catch the ball at the base of the shaft with your thumb.

1. Once the ball is on your sidewall, start by holding the stick in your strong hand at the base of the shaft.

2. Rotate your wrist upward so that the head of your stick moves slowly toward the sky. This will allow the ball to roll down the shaft toward your hand. This step relies on balance. Make sure that the ball rolls straight; otherwise, it will deviate from the shaft.

3. Free your thumb from the grip you are holding, and just as the ball is about to meet your hand, stop the ball with your thumb for the catch.

THE TRICK

A player defies gravity by popping the ball to herself, bringing her stick over and then under the ball, and catching the ball, all before the ball hits the ground.

EXECUTION

1. Begin by holding the stick and ball with two hands, parallel to the ground, in front of your body. Next, pop the ball up toward the center of your chest to about heart level.

2. While the ball is in the air, quickly bring your stick over the top of the falling ball and swiftly back under it in a circular motion (push upward and then downward). In order to complete the trick correctly, come over and under the ball with two hands on the stick. The ball must travel in between your arms and hands.

3. After you have come underneath the ball, swiftly shift your stick so that the head of the stick comes underneath the ball for the catch.

(continued)

COACHING POINT

Make sure the player has the ball between her hands when doing step 2. Too often players think they have completed the trick by simply circling the falling ball with the head of the stick.

VARIATION

Once you have completed the Over and Under trick, you can reverse it and go under and then over the falling ball. You must do this one faster, however, because it is more difficult.

THE TRICK

This trick involves a series of stick skills that when put together create a fluid routine that increases stick awareness.

EXECUTION

1. Flick to yourself: Begin by holding the stick and ball in your strong hand. Use your wrist to flick the ball straight up and catch it at your side.

2. Behind the back flick: From there, flip the ball to your opposite hip. Then bring the stick behind your back and catch where you just flicked the ball.

3. Flick out: Catch the ball behind your back. Then flick it from there back in front and catch it.

4. Between the legs: The ball is now directly in front of you. Flick the ball up in the air. This time, bring your stick behind you and between your legs to catch the ball.

5. Over and under pass: Flick the ball up to about eye level from between your legs. Then bring the stick back around in front of you. While the ball is in the air, bring your stick over the ball in a swimming motion. Come underneath the ball so that the head of the stick is pointing toward your body and catch the ball.

6. Catch behind: Continue the catch between your legs. Once the stick with the ball is between your legs, almost like a tail, flick the ball up toward your weak-hand shoulder.

7. Follow the ball: Follow the ball with your eye as it flicks over your shoulder and catch it underhand in front of your body.

COACHING POINT

Each of these steps is easier the more a player chokes up on her stick.

VARIATIONS

Around the World

Once you have mastered the steps described previously, you can add a one-handed Around the World. Bring your stick across your body and wrap your arm around your front side so that the stick is underneath your weak-hand shoulder. Combine that motion with an upward flick and catch the ball in front of you.

With a Partner

You can also do all of these steps simultaneously with a partner. Instead of flicking a pass to yourself in steps 6 and 7, you and your partner can flick a pass to each other.

(continued)

(continued)

Conditioning Drills

One of the most important elements of execution on the lacrosse field is focus. Fatigued players find it particularly challenging to focus, but those who can focus when tired have an advantage over the other players. Drills that force players to focus and execute when they are tired will reinforce the skill. Any drill will become a conditioning drill if players execute it at full speed and at their highest intensity. The following drills are particularly intensive. If players are able to execute skills and concepts at full speed throughout a full practice, they will be fit enough to execute during a game.

PURPOSE

This drill works on transition passes and moving the ball down the field quickly. It also allows the goalie to be incorporated into a passing drill.

SETUP

Players form four equal lines in 20-yard (18.3 m) increments down each sideline (a total of eight lines). Goalies are in the goal at both ends.

EXECUTION

1. The goalie clears to the first line on one side.

2. The first player in line catches the ball and passes to the first player in the second line on the other side of the field.

3. The first player in the second line catches the ball and passes it to the first player in the third line on the other side of the field.

4. The first player in that line catches the ball and passes to the last (fourth) line on the opposite side of the field. This player takes a shot on goal to end the set.

5. The original goalie restarts the drill with a clear to the other side. The ball continues down the field as it is passed diagonally from line to line (four passes including the clear); each set ends with a shot on goal from the last line. The goalie alternates which side she clears to each time. The drill should be continuous.

COACHING POINT

Make sure players are going at full speed. This drill has built-in conditioning. If the team is doing well, add a trailing defender (the defender must always stay behind and look for back checks).

PURPOSE

This drill allows players to work continuously on odd-man breaks; it also serves as a team conditioning drill.

SETUP

The team divides into two groups. The goals are positioned 40 to 50 yards (35.6-45.7 m) apart. Each team forms three equal lines along their goal line.

EXECUTION

1. One team is designated to be on defense first. Two players from this team step out.

2. The first three players on the opposite team step out and receive a clear from their goalie to start the drill.

3. The three attackers go to goal on a 3v2 against the other team.

4. The 3v2 ends as soon as the ball is thrown away, a goal is scored, a save is made, or a turnover is caused.

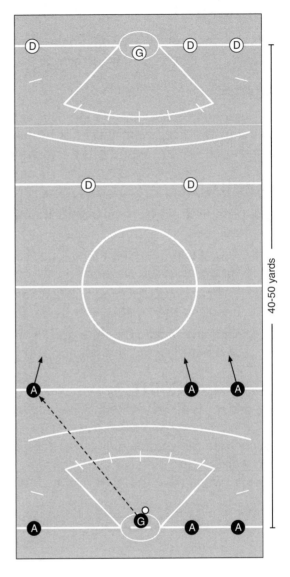

5. The last attacker to touch the ball drops out and returns to her team's line.

6. The remaining two attackers become the defenders. The other team (originally the defensive team) sends out three new attackers who receive a clear from their goalie and go to goal on their own 3v2.

7. This pattern continues over and over.

COACHING POINT

Make this a competitive drill for your team. Have them play up to 20 goals for a certain amount of time (10-minute halves or other timing). This makes the drill more intense and more fun.

PURPOSE

This drill addresses stickwork on the move—passing, cradling, receiving—and includes conditioning. Players need to be able to execute stickwork when tired.

SETUP

The team is divided into groups of seven to nine. The players in each group split into two lines, with the front of the lines facing each other. One player stands halfway between the two lines and acts as the passer.

EXECUTION

1. The first player runs toward the other line and passes the ball to the passer.
2. The passer receives the ball and immediately passes back to the player for a give-and-go.
3. The player receives the ball and passes to the first player in the opposite line, who then follows the same steps in the other direction.
4. This drill should be done quickly and consistently. After a while, switch another player to the passer position.

COACHING POINT

The drill must be done on the move with no stationary passing. The fewer players in each line, the harder the drill becomes from a conditioning standpoint. To increase the conditioning level, decrease the number of players in the line and increase the distance between the two lines. To increase the difficulty of the stickwork, have the players switch hands or receive the ball offside.

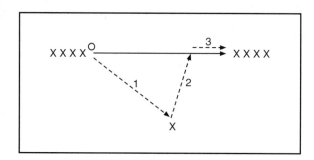

PURPOSE

Shooting takes considerable focus. Shooters have a limited number of scoring opportunities in a game, and they need to be able to capitalize on these opportunities. Practicing shooting when players are tired will increase their ability to execute scoring opportunities in a game.

EXECUTION

Use any of the shooting drills listed in the Shooting Drills section of chapter 10 and add sprint repetitions between each set. For example, after the shooter takes a shot or a series of shots, have her sprint to the 50-yard line before getting back in line. The distance and number of sprints can be adjusted to increase or decrease the conditioning level.

PURPOSE

Sliding is one of the most important defensive concepts, and players must become comfortable with sliding in any direction, at any time, even when they are tired. Defenders also must keep their heads up and follow directions from their goalie or supporting teammates.

SETUP

Defensive players line up in the defensive zone or anywhere on the field. A coach is 15 yards (13.7 m) ahead of them with a stick.

EXECUTION

1. The coach points the stick in different directions: left, right, forward, and back.
2. The defensive players slide in whatever direction the stick points.
3. The drill continues for as long as the coach continues to point the stick.

COACHING POINT

The longer this drill is done, the more conditioning intensive it will become. To make the drill more challenging, players can start by lying down on the field. When the coach points the stick, the players jump up and slide in the designated direction. Slides should be done quickly, and players should keep their sticks up in a defensive position.

PURPOSE

Many offensive opportunities arise from 1v1 situations, and many offensive plays are built around setting up a 1v1 for an attacker. Both the attacker and defender must be well conditioned to execute a 1v1.

SETUP

Groups of two players set up at each hash around the 8-meter area; one is designated the attacker and has the ball, and the other is the defender.

EXECUTION

1. The attacker on the first hash tries to beat the defender to goal.
2. The defender tries to contain the attacker, force a bad shot, or create a turnover.
3. Immediately after the 1v1 ends, the attacker on the next hash moves to goal.
4. The drill is repeated with each attacker all the way around the 8-meter area. Players should rotate from attack to defense.

COACHING POINT

This drill can be done at both ends of the field. The fewer the players in each line, the more repetitions each player will get, and the more conditioning intensive the drill becomes.

PURPOSE

Players need to work on executing shots when fatigued. Scoring opportunities are limited, and this drill can simulate a conditioning- and footwork-intensive situation after which a player must focus and execute a shot on goal.

SETUP

The coach sets up two agility ladders starting at the 50-yard line. The team is split into two lines, one behind each of the agility ladders. There are balls in each line and a goalie in the net.

EXECUTION

1. The coach designates a specific footwork drill to be done through the agility ladder. For example, players may have to put one foot in a square, two feet in the next square, one foot in the next, and so on.
2. The first player in line goes through the agility ladder while cradling the ball in her stick; she then runs to goal and takes a shot.
3. When the first player is halfway through the ladder, the first player in the other line begins.
4. The lines alternate as each player goes through the ladder and takes shots on goal.

COACHING POINT

The drill becomes more challenging with fewer players in each line and if the distance from the end of the ladder to the goal is increased. Make sure the players focus on correctly executing both the footwork in the agility ladder and the shot on goal.

PURPOSE

Offensive dodges become increasingly challenging as a player gets tired. A player must execute her dodges at full speed—both footwork and stickwork—for the dodge to be effective and prevent the defense from causing a turnover.

SETUP

Players with balls line up on the end line.

EXECUTION

1. Players execute their dodges, over and over again, all the way to the other side of the field.
2. This drill can be repeated with any dodge: face dodge, split dodge, roll dodge, and so on.

COACHING POINT

To make the drill more challenging, add a defender in front of the attacker. The attacker will be forced to dodge at full speed and intensity with a defender who is trying to cause a turnover playing in front of her.

PURPOSE

As described in chapter 8, handling ground balls is one of the most important elements of a game; it's based almost entirely on hard work and determination. As a game progresses and players become increasingly tired, the player who is able to work hard for the ground ball and come up with it will be at a significant advantage.

SETUP

Players set up in two lines at the 50-yard line, with a coach in the middle. Both lines face the goal.

EXECUTION

1. The coach throws the ground ball in any direction, and the first player in each of the two lines runs out and competes for the ground ball.
2. Whoever picks up the ball becomes the attacker, and whoever does not becomes the defender.
3. The attacker then takes the defender 1v1 to goal.
4. After the 1v1 is finished, the coach rolls out the next ball. This drill can be done with multiple players to create a 2v2, 3v3, and so on.

COACHING POINT

The drill becomes more challenging with fewer players in each line and the greater the distance from the lines to the goal. The drill can be done on both sides of the field to split the team into four groups. As you add players to the drill (e.g., 3v3), the time between repetitions will decrease, and the drill will become more challenging.

PURPOSE

This drill emphasizes stickwork—passing and catching—and footwork. Even when players become increasingly more tired, they still need to be able to execute their stickwork, make crisp passes, and catch the ball.

SETUP

Players split into groups of three. One player is in the middle with the outside two players facing the player in the middle, about 10 yards (9.1 m) away from her. One of the outside players starts with the ball.

EXECUTION

1. The player in the middle cuts toward the player with the ball and receives the pass.
2. The player in the middle then pivots toward the other player and passes to her.
3. The player in the middle then recuts, receives the ball from the player she just passed to, pivots, and passes back to the other player.
4. The player in the middle repeats this pattern, going back and forth between passing and receiving with each player.
5. The players then rotate so that another player goes into the middle position.

COACHING POINT

The longer each player stays in the middle, the more conditioning intensive the drill becomes. To make the drill more challenging, force players to use their weak hands, catch offside, throw offside, fake before they pass, and so on.

Maximizing Practice Time

Because any team has only a limited amount of time to work together, a coach needs to maximize the allotted practice time. This chapter addresses certain components and organizational methods that will help develop efficient practices. Toward the end of the chapter are five practice plans of various lengths that might serve as models or guidelines.

Components and Organization

Team practices should begin with a warm-up and progress from focused skill practice and drills to bigger-picture concepts and full-field scenarios. When a team becomes comfortable with an isolated skill or concept, they will be better able to apply the concept in a game situation. The game of lacrosse is built on many skills and concepts, and it is important to break each concept down for players to achieve a cumulative understanding of the game.

A coach needs to prepare a specific plan when he or she goes into a practice; however, the coach must be flexible and ready to change the plan based on what the team seems to need that specific day, how well they execute, how they respond to drills, and how quickly they progress.

Another way to maximize practice sessions is to build in competition. Competition creates excitement, forces players to practice at game speed, introduces a level of accountability, and helps create a gamelike atmosphere in practice.

The following sections explain each segment of a practice session.

Warm-Ups   Every practice should begin with a full warm-up. A warm-up gets players moving and focused and, most important, it helps prevent injury. A warm-up should begin with a short, relatively low-intensity run—a simple lap or two around the field. Players should then stretch for 7 to 10 minutes. In addition to having players run and stretch, it is important to add dynamic elements such as plyometrics to the warm-up. The term *plyometrics* refers to a type of exercise that uses explosive and muscle-intensive movements, such as high knees, walking lunges, or body-weight squats. Plyos warm up players' muscles and prepare the players to transition into full-speed practice drills.

Stickwork   Players need to have opportunities to work on their stickwork at every practice. Stickwork is the most fundamental element of lacrosse, and the more a player practices her stickwork, the more she will become comfortable and able to execute stickwork in a game situation. Even at the highest level of the game, players need to practice stickwork consistently. There is always room to improve. Partner passing allows players to warm up their sticks, work on new skills, and improve their stickwork. Coaches can use this time to incorporate specific stickwork concepts that will be used in drills as the practice progresses. For example, if the coach plans to run a passing drill that includes catching offside and passing with both hands, the stickwork portion of practice can focus on these specific skills before incorporating them into a full drill. This is also a good time for the goalies to begin warming up.

Position-Specific Drills   After players have worked on their stickwork, the team can move into drills that work on specific skills and microlevel concepts such as shooting, passing, defensive body position, and goalie skills. Players need to master these skills before executing bigger concepts. Players can work on them in an isolated fashion before doing a drill that requires and incorporates those skills in a more complex situation.

Small-Sided Concept Drills   Small-sided concept drills work on specific pieces of the full game. For example, 2v2s and 3v2s incorporate pieces of the larger, gamelike 7v7 attack versus defense situation. It is helpful for players to practice movement and positioning with fewer players before putting all the pieces together. Another example of a small-sided concept drill is one that focuses on the team's transition out of the defensive zone and into the midfield: The team can work on the first two or three transition passes and build up to a full-field transition.

Big Concept Drills   Big concept drills should incorporate small-sided concepts into a specific team's game plan. They should also build on and integrate stickwork, position-specific skills, and small-sided concepts. Big concept drills put all of the microlevel pieces together to emphasize a specific aspect of the game: attacking plays, defensive plays, transition offense, or transition defense. Big concept drills are most effective when the team has already become comfortable with the smaller pieces that make up the big picture.

Scrimmage   A full-field scrimmage is a tool in determining how well a team is able to execute the various skills and concepts that have been practiced. Full-field play gives players an opportunity to put everything together and provides a measuring stick for a coach to judge the team's execution. Scrimmages are also a good way to implement competition and create a gamelike atmosphere in practice.

Cool-Down and Stretch   After an intense practice, or any practice, players need time to cool down and stretch their muscles to prevent soreness, tightness, and injury.

Sample Practice Plans

Refer to chapters 10 and 12 for drills.

Plan A: 2.5 Hours

- Warm-up (15-20 minutes)
- Stickwork (30 minutes)
  - Partner passing
    - Strong hand
    - Weak hand
    - Offside catch, strong-side pass
    - Offside catch, weak-side pass
    - Bounce passes
    - Behind-the-back passes
    - One-handed catch, strong-side pass
    - Strong-side fake, offside pass
  - Stationary protection drill
- Position-specific drills (20 minutes)
  - Protection on the move
  - Basic shooting shuttle
  - Four corners shooting drill
- Small-sided concept drills (30 minutes)
  - Protection in double-team
  - 1v1 off the pass
  - 3v2 from restraining line
  - 4v4 attacking motion
- Big concept drills (30 minutes)
  - Attacking plays
  - Defensive setups (man-to-man, zone, high pressure, and so on)
  - Settled attack and settled defense
- Scrimmage (25 minutes)

Plan B: 2.5 Hours

- Warm-up (15-20 minutes)
- Stickwork (30 minutes)
  - Partner passing
    - Strong hand
    - Weak hand
    - Offside catch, strong-side pass
    - Offside catch, weak-side pass
    - Bounce passes
    - Behind-the-back passes
    - One-handed catch, strong-side pass
    - Strong-side fake, offside pass
  - Stationary protection drill
- Position-specific drills (20 minutes)
  - Give-and-go drill
  - Cutting off the pick
  - Three-line shooting drill
- Small-sided concept drills (30 minutes)
  - 2v2 picking plays
  - 3v2 in tight
  - 4v3 defensive box drill
- Big concept drills (30 minutes)
  - 7v7
  - Full-field transition (from attack to defense, from defense to attack)
- Scrimmage (25 minutes)
- Cool-down and stretch

Plan C: 90 Minutes

- Warm-up (15 minutes)
- Stickwork (20 minutes)
  - Partner passing
    - Strong hand
    - Weak hand
    - Offside catch, strong-side pass
    - Offside catch, weak-side pass
    - Bounce passes
    - Behind-the-back passes
    - One-handed catch, strong-side pass
    - Strong-side fake, offside pass
  - 3-man on the move: passing variation
- Position-specific drills (15 minutes)
  - 3-man on the move: protection variation
  - Four corners shooting drill
- Small-sided concept drills (20 minutes)
  - 1v1 off the pass
  - Attacking plays: clear space for 1v1
- Big concept drills (20 minutes)
  - 3v2 continuous

Plan D: 90 Minutes

- Warm-up (15 minutes)
- Stickwork (20 minutes)
  - Partner passing
    - Strong hand
    - Weak hand
    - Offside catch, strong-side pass
    - Offside catch, weak-side pass
    - Bounce passes
    - Behind-the-back passes
    - One-handed catch, strong-side pass
    - Strong-side fake, offside pass
  - Stationary protection drill
- Position-specific drills (15 minutes)
  - Protection in double-team
  - Three-line shooting drill
- Small-sided concept drills (20 minutes)
  - Competitive ground balls
  - 3v2 breakout drill
- Big concept drills (20 minutes)
  - Scrimmage

Plan E: 60 Minutes

- Warm-up (15 minutes)
- Stickwork (15 minutes)
  - Partner passing
    - Strong hand
    - Weak hand
    - Offside catch, strong-side pass
    - Offside catch, weak-side pass
    - Bounce passes
    - Behind-the-back passes
    - One-handed catch, strong-side pass
    - Strong-side fake, offside pass
  - Middleman passing drill
- Position-specific drills (10 minutes)
  - Basic shooting shuttle
  - Cutting off the pick
- Small-sided concept drills (10 minutes)
  - 3v2 in tight
  - 3v2 from the 50-yard line
- Big concept drills (10 minutes)
  - 7v7 at both ends of the field

About the Author

Kelly Amonte Hiller has served as the head women's lacrosse coach at Northwestern University since 2001. During her time at Northwestern, Amonte Hiller has transformed a club level team into an NCAA Division I dynasty, and amassed a 134-24 overall record. In that span, she has won five consecutive NCAA national championships and an unprecedented 106-3 record in her championship seasons. Amonte Hiller was named American Lacrosse Conference Coach of the Year in 2004, 2005, 2006, 2007, and 2009. Before joining the coaching staff at Northwestern University, Amonte Hiller was an assistant coach at Brown, Umass, and Boston University.

Amonte Hiller played college lacrosse for the University of Maryland where she was a four-time All-American standout and won back to back IWLCA National Player of the Year honors. She was also named the 1996 ACC Female Athlete of the Year. After her college career, Kelly played for the U.S. national team, where she was a member of the 1997 and 2001 World Cup championship teams.